The Most Awful
The Most Underhanded Deals.
The Biggest Financial Fiascoes Are All In...

THE MISFORTUNE 500™

WORST BUSINESS DECISION BY A RECORD COMPANY

In 1962, Decca Recording refused to sign a group named The Beatles, saying, "Groups with guitars are on their way out."

THE MOST EXPLOSIVE NEW PRODUCT

It was billed as Napa Natural — the first all-natural soft drink. The problem: Natural juice ferments, and cans of Napa Natural literally exploded into the marketplace — on supermarket shelves!

CHARTER MEMBER OF THE BUSINESS HALL OF SHAME

J. Paul Getty, who controlled the flushing of his company's toilets in order to save money.

WORST PROMOTIONAL GIMMICK

United Airline's "Fly Your Wife Free" campaign. Thousands of businessmen took up the offer. United sent thank-you letters to their wives — and thousands of wives wrote back, demanding to know who had been flying with their husbands!

THE MOST OFFENSIVE ADVERTISING HEADLINE

"IT TAKES MORE THAN BIG CHESTS AND NICE JUGS TO ATTRACT CUSTOMERS." From an advertisement for King-Seely Thermos Company.

IT'S AMERICAN BUSINESS AT ITS HILARIOUS WORST, IN...
THE MISFORTUNE 500™

Books by Bruce Nash and Allan Zullo

The Baseball Hall of Shame™
The Baseball Hall of Shame 2™
The Baseball Hall of Shame 3™
The Football Hall of Shame™
The Sports Hall of Shame™
Baseball Confidential™
The Misfortune 500™

Published by POCKET BOOKS

Most Pocket Books are available at special quantity discounts for bulk purchases for sales promotions, premiums or fund raising. Special books or book excerpts can also be created to fit specific needs.

For details write the office of the Vice President of Special Markets, Pocket Books, 1230 Avenue of the Americas, New York, New York 10020.

THE MIS-FORTUNE 500™

FEATURING THE BUSINESS HALL OF SHAME™

BRUCE NASH AND ALLAN ZULLO

CARTOONS BY BILL MAUL

POCKET BOOKS

New York   London   Toronto   Sydney   Tokyo

This book is dedicated to our fathers, Murray Nash and Anthony Zullo, who learned how to conduct business the right way and who were convinced we could run anything—except their businesses.

An *Original* publication of POCKET BOOKS

POCKET BOOKS, A Division of Simon & Schuster Inc., 1230 Avenue of the Americas, New York, N.Y. 10020

Copyright © 1988 by Nash and Zullo Productions, Inc.
Cover artwork copyright © 1988 Jack Davis

The Misfortune 500 and The Business Hall of Shame are trademarks of Nash and Zullo Productions, Inc.

All rights reserved, including the right to reproduce this book or portions thereof in any form whatsoever. For information address Pocket Books, 1230 Avenue of the Americas, New York, N.Y. 10020

ISBN: 0-671-63733-9

First Pocket Books trade paperback printing: June, 1988

10 9 8 7 6 5 4 3 2 1

POCKET and colophon are trademarks of Simon & Schuster Inc.

Printed in the U.S.A.

CONTENTS

Memorandum	viii
THE MISMANAGEMENT TEAM	1
THE UNBALANCED SHEET	13
PRODUCTS OF A WARPED IMAGINATION	21
CAPITALIZING CAPITALISTS	29
CHIEF EGOMANIACS AND OPPRESSORS (CEOs)	33
LOOKING OUT FOR NO. 1	39
THE BUSINESS HALL OF SHAME	47
DEPRECIATING THE COMPANY	53
ALL HYPED UP	61
DEMOTIONS FOR PROMOTIONS	75
BADVERTISING CAMPAIGNS	85
UNTRUTH IN ADVERTISING	95

CUSTOMER DISSERVICE	107
IMPERSONNEL RELATIONS	117
THE RANK AND VILE	129
FUNNY BUSINESS	137
DOUBLE STANDARD BEARERS	145
BELOW THE LINE	151
NO-ACCOUNT ACCOUNTING	173
A CROCK FOR YOUR STOCK	179
*ART*FUL DODGERS	189
WHO'S WHO IN THE MISFORTUNE 500	199
WHO ELSE BELONGS IN THE MISFORTUNE 500?	209

ACKNOWLEDGMENT

We wish to thank the following for their assistance: Robert McMath and Janet Mansfield, Marketing Intelligence Service Ltd.; Diane Bratcher, Interfaith Center on Corporate Responsibility; Carol Davis, Industrial Union Department, AFL-CIO; Richard Lewis, Corporate Annual Reports, Inc.; Sid Cato, *Sid Cato's Newsletter on Annual Reports;* Chris Lee, *Training* magazine; William Lutz, *Quarterly Review of Doublespeak;* Flora Muniz, *Marketing Week;* Bruce Silverglade, Dora Demmings, and D'Anne DuBois, Center for Science in the Public Interest; Lewis Gilbert, John Gilbert, Bernadette Liberti, and David Brown, Corporate Democracy Inc.; Clarence Ditlow, Center for Auto Safety; J. P. Donon, *Chief Executive;* Robert Levy, *Dun's Business Month;* and *American Banker.*

Special thanks go to our friend and top-flight researcher Bernie Ward and to our greatest assets—our families: Sophie, Robyn, and Jennifer Nash; and Kathy, Allison, and Sasha Zullo.

Memorandum

To: The Reader
From: The Authors
Re: The Misfortune 500

The annals of business are filled with so many red-inked accounts of goofs and gaffes that the business world must have spawned Murphy's Law: If something can go wrong, it will—and at the worst possible time.

More than 50,000 companies go belly-up every year and tens of thousands of other corporations screw up in some fashion. Nevertheless, blunders don't get the attention they deserve. Neither do the zany and embarrassing moments that result from outrageous boners, bizarre business practices, and absurd decisions. Companies just don't want to talk about them.

The tenants of executive suites and the climbers of corporate ladders are so obsessed with success that they can't even say the words "failure" or "mistake," much less laugh at such incidents—unless, of course, the words refer to their competitors. Uptight execs prefer to stay mum and bury their heads in books about motivation and excellence.

But you are about to read a business book that puts all others to shame. The Misfortune 500 goes beyond the bottom line of the business world—beyond Edsel, new Coke, and the Hunt brothers. From the boardrooms to the stockrooms, from the multinational to the hometown bank, from the corporate fast track to the corporate Vietnam, we have discovered that business people have the propensity to embarrass themselves, usually with funny consequences.

At least we thought they were funny. Unfortunately, the titans of industry and commerce found nothing amusing about our quest for real-life ignoble incidents in business. We wrote to the CEOs of thirty-five of our nation's top corporations asking each for a five-minute phone conversation at their convenience day or night to tell us one true, humorous story about business. Not a single CEO cooperated. Most didn't even have the courtesy to respond. Those who did answer told us—through their corporate relations people—that they had better things to do. The letters were brief messages similar to this one sent by V. E. Pesqueira, manager of executive communications for

Xerox Corp., who wrote, "Thanks for your offer, but I'm afraid we'll have to decline. There probably isn't a CEO in the world as nice and as approachable as David Kearns—but he would hate it." C. R. Walgreen III was the only chairman who took the time to personally write us a note. He minced no words: "I appreciate your inviting me to participate, but would have no interest in doing so."

We can't say we were surprised. We just wrote it off as a loss and scoured business publications, interviewed corporate consultants and consumer advocates, contacted industry associations and business schools, pored over annual reports, examined proxy statements, and read news accounts. We called companies to verify the facts, but only succeeded in giving anxiety attacks to dozens of corporate relations vice-presidents who were slow to talk and quick to hang up.

Nevertheless, we collected hundreds of true stories of business practices that were usually hilarious, often wacky, and sometimes startling. We found 500 companies and individuals who fouled up. However, they are not the only ones—just the unlucky ones who caught our attention. The MISFORTUNE 500 is not a ranking of the worst failures, mistakes, or business practices in history. Rather it is a primer on how *not* to conduct business.

What's in a Name?

Because of mergers, takeovers, and boardroom whim, companies are constantly changing their names.

Look what happened to United Airlines—a perfectly fine name. It eventually became UAL and then in May 1987, it was changed to Allegis (a combination of the words "allegiance" and "aegis"). After spending $7.3 million for the name change, the company announced it would shuck the new moniker in 1988 and return to its original name.

Several companies mentioned in this book have changed their names. In writing about these companies, we used the names that they were known by at the time the incidents took place.

THE MISMANAGEMENT TEAM

MALFEASANCE IN THE CORPOCRACY

Generous to a Fault

When Du Pont wanted to trim its 100,000-employee U.S. work force in 1985, the company offered a generous early retirement program to all but its top managers. It wanted to avoid the hardship of layoffs but instead created a hardship for itself.

Intending to trim personnel by about 5 percent, Du Pont and its subsidary, Conoco Inc., expected about 6,000 employees to cash in on the deal. The company promised to add five years to both the age and service records of employees who left early. As a result, the pension of a 55-year-old employee with a salary of $25,000 and 30 years' experience was treated as though he were 60 and had put in 35 years. That meant his pension would be $817 a month instead of $595.

The terms were far more attractive than the company realized. More than 11,000—nearly 10 percent of those eligible—took the money and ran. At Conoco, 2,000 workers, just over 10 percent of those eligible, chose to leave—and the exodus ran to 16.5 percent at some refineries. Complained Conoco president Dino Nicandros, "There are some people taking the offer we wish hadn't."

The retirement plan cost Du Pont $125 million in 1985. Yet it was really much more costly than that. The company had to offer bonuses to valued employees to keep them on the job and also had to hire new people and transfer others to fill some crucial vacancies.

What We Have Here Is a Failure to Communicate

In 1968, the Chevrolet promotions department had a brainstorm: Let's launch a major advertising campaign to hype the four-cylinder Nova, said the promo people. We'll place big ads in newspapers, run TV and radio commercials, and support dealer promotions with traditional bright-colored banners.

Everyone at Chevrolet was told about the plan except the good folks in Chevy's manufacturing division, who had a brainstorm of their own: Let's de-emphasize four-cylinder engine production because sales had fallen off, they said. We'll take most of the four-cylinder equipment out of the plants. And so they did.

Meanwhile, Chevy management never bothered to see if the four-cylinder Novas that were being promoted could in fact be built.

Management found out all too soon. The manufacturing division was overwhelmed. The number of engine orders was six times more than the division's production capability. Everyone got burned. Chevrolet couldn't meet the dealer orders. The dealers couldn't supply the cars that the customers ordered. And the customers didn't get the cars that Chevy's own advertising had convinced them they wanted.

The Bill and Mary Datebook of Events

June, 1979: **Bill Agee**, 41-year-old president of Bendix, hires 28-year-old **Mary Cunningham**—a willowy blonde fresh out of the Harvard Business School—as his executive assistant.

June, 1980: Finding Mary a skilled (not to mention attractive) businesswoman, Bill names her Vice President for Corporate and Public Affairs. Mary becomes the youngest female corporate vice president among the Fortune 500 companies. This leads tongues to wagging at the Bendix water coolers because Mary and Bill have been constantly together lunching, working, and jetting around the country.

August, 1980: Anonymous letters are sent to the Bendix board urging board members to investigate the relationship between Bill and Mary. More letters reach Detroit newspaper editors, but they have too little to go on—yet.

Labor Day, 1980: It is confirmed that Bill and his wife have divorced.

One Week Later: Bill promotes Mary again, this time to Vice President for Strategic Planning.

Two Weeks Later: At an annual meeting of Bendix's 600 executives, attended by reporters, Bill discusses short-term and long-range company goals—and then confronts the rumors head on: "I've been told by many people, and I know that it is buzzing around, that Mary Cunningham's rise in this company is very unusual and that it has something to do with a personal relationship we have. Sure, it's unusual. Her rise in this company is unusual because she's a very talented individual. But her rapid promotions are totally justified." But Bill gives even more credence to the rumors by adding, "I tell you it is true that we are very, very close friends, and she's a very close friend of my family. But that has absolutely nothing to do with the way that I and others in this company and on the board evaluate her performance."

The Next Day: The newspapers finally have a peg on the rumors and run a page-one story headlined: BENDIX BOSS SLAPS DOWN OFFICE GOSSIP, FEMALE EXEC'S RISE NOT DUE TO FRIENDSHIP, AGEE TELLS STAFF. Said the story, "It was an unusual moment in corporate America—a chief executive giving rumors the status of company concerns that needed to be discussed openly with subordinates." Meanwhile, Mary is asked by an uncouth reporter, "So, how long have you been sleeping with the boss?"

October 1980: Members of the Bendix board insist that Bill fire Mary. He can't do it. Instead, Mary resigns from Bendix.

April 1982: Bill discovers that being linked romantically with Mary over the past year and a half is his Achilles' heel. Following a strategy that Mary helped refine when she was at Bendix, Bill tries to acquire a major high-tech firm. He begins to purchase stock in RCA for a possible hostile takeover. Suddenly, a pro-RCA press release is issued that says Bill "has not demonstrated his ability to manage his own affairs, let alone someone else's." Bill leaves RCA alone.

June 1982: Bill and Mary wed.

September 1982: Acting on Mary's advice, Bill tries to engineer a Bendix takeover of Martin Marietta. But Martin Marietta launches a Pac-Man defense and tries to take over Bendix. Then Allied Corp. enters the picture and offers to buy *both* companies. When the dealmaking ends, Bendix is owned by Allied, Marietta remains an independent company, and *Time* magazine calls the whole thing "Merger Theater of the Absurd."

1983: Bill leaves Allied in a huff. He and Mary buy a Cape Cod home and form their own investment company named Semper—Latin for "always."

Seven Symptoms of Mismanagement at Allegheny International

(Or Why Chairman Robert J. Buckley Resigned in 1986)

1. The Pittsburgh-based consumer products company lost $164 million in 1986, topping the previous year's financial bath of $109 million in losses.

2. AI provided its top executives personal use of a fleet of five jets dubbed the "Allegheny Air Force."

3. AI granted more than $30 million in personal loans to executives at only 2 percent interest.

4. Sons and daughters of senior executives were placed on the payroll. One of the chairman's sons was appointed manager of an AI-owned Manhattan hotel, even though he had no hotel management experience.

5. A dummy corporation set up by AI in 1985 spent nearly $1 million for the purchase and furnishing of a swank Tudor home in Pittsburgh to entertain directors and important clients.

6. AI took a huge writeoff after bankrolling the $80 million construction of a Houston office building. The company rejected an offer that would have recouped the investment in 1983 and instead let the building stand vacant for two years—at a carrying cost of $1 million a month—before selling it in 1985 for $47 million.

7. Chairman Robert J. Buckley appointed as investor relations manager a math teacher who tutored his children.

Imagine If They Had Made a Profit

How Slumping Companies Reward Their Bigwigs

LTV CORP.

When LTV suffered a whopping $378.2 million loss in 1984, it lent chairman and CEO Raymond Hay nearly $1 million so he could exercise expiring stock options. According to the loan agreement, Hay, who received nearly $750,000 in salary, wouldn't have to pay interest on the five-year loan as long as he kept his job.

What made the loan so outrageous was that earlier in the year, the company closed a steel plant rather than accept a United Steel Workers Union proposal to give workers preferred stock in exchange for contract concessions of $6 an hour. The amount LTV advanced to Hay would have been more than enough to cover the preferred stock and save the operation's 600 jobs.

AMERICAN MOTORS CORP.

American Motors could have learned something from the Japanese automakers who trimmed their top executives' pay when profits declined as the result of the strengthening yen in 1985. However, even though American Motors piled up $125.3 million in losses that year, it substantially boosted the salaries of its three top executives by at least 23 percent.

PETRO-LEWIS CORP.

In 1984, Petro-Lewis recorded a $54 million loss. So what did the Denver-based energy concern do to chairman Jerome Lewis? Citing his "outstanding performance," the company gave Lewis $163,000 in bonuses and $1.1 million in cash for an old stock option. Petro-Lewis allowed him to choose cash equaling the difference between the option's exercise price and the stock's market value rather than accept the shares.

"It's shocking that he would line his pockets [with the stock option] while people who entrusted him with their money were getting killed," one irate investor told *The Wall Street Journal*. A spokeswoman for Petro-Lewis showed her compassion by telling the *Journal*, "Yes, a million dollars looks like a lot to some individuals, but in the scope of things, would that amount really have made a difference?"

TGI FRIDAY'S INC.

While profits of the restaurant chain fell 20 percent in 1985, the company gave CEO Daniel Scoggin a salary package that included a 10 percent raise plus 20 percent of the pretax income from a new fast-food concept. TGI Friday's also let Scoggin exercise a put option that brought him an additional $3.5 million. And just to be extra nice, the company chipped in $25,000 toward Scoggin's purchase of a new $96,500 Rolls-Royce.

CHARTER CO.

In February 1984, the oil and insurance company rewarded twenty-seven top executives with $3.8 million in "special incentive bonuses." Five top officers received $250,000 each. Two months later, Charter entered Chapter 11 bankruptcy proceedings.

UAL INC.

Despite red ink, UAL saw fit to keep chairman Richard J. Ferris in the pink with plenty of green. In 1985, the company racked up losses of $48.7 million. For this stunningly bad performance, UAL didn't cut his pay accordingly, but doubled it to $883,000.

COCA-COLA CO.

Rather than criticize its top two executives for an infamous strategic boner, Coke rewarded them. In 1985, the company's compensation committee granted chairman Roberto Goizueta and president Donald Keough new benefits potentially worth millions of dollars for their "courage, wisdom, and commitment" in introducing new Coke, the year's biggest new-product flop!

If It Ain't Broke, Don't Fix It

NEW COKE ISN'T IT

In May 1985, when Coca-Cola announced it had fiddled with the formula for its ninety-nine-year-old beverage, the company quickly discovered that changing the world's best-selling soda was the marketing blunder of the decade.

Hoping to reverse rival Pepsi's steady gains in market share, Coca-Cola chairman Roberto Goizueta and president Donald Keough decided in 1982 that their company should create a new and sweeter soda. After three years of exhaustive taste tests, Coca-Cola introduced a reformulated new Coke.

New Coke was met with fury from tens of thousands of Coke lovers who reviled the suddenly sweeter taste of their favorite beverage and demanded old Coke back. For three straight months, Coca-Cola headquarters received about 1,500 phone calls daily and tons of mail from angry protestors.

"The passion for original Coke was something that just flat caught us by surprise," a chastened Keough confessed to the press. "The simple fact is that all of the time and money and skill poured into consumer research on the new Coca-Cola could not measure or reveal the depth and emotional attachment to the original Coca-Cola felt by so many people."

Keough denied that new Coke was a plot to create support for the older product. "Some critics will say Coca-Cola has made a marketing mistake. Some cynics say that we planned the whole thing. The truth is, we're not that dumb, and we're not that smart."

In one of the most spectacular about-faces in American business, the company bowed to public pressure. Within two months, it declared that old Coke would be restored to groceries, fountains, and vending machines. The old Coke soon returned as Coca-Cola Classic while the new Coke that ignited the outrage remained as the flagship brand.

Coca-Cola's big fizzle was summed up by Roger Enrico, president of Pepsi-Cola USA, who crowed: "Clearly this is the Edsel of the eighties. This was a terrible mistake. Coke's got a lemon on its hands, and now they're trying to make lemonade."

BREWING TROUBLE AT SCHLITZ

If Coca-Cola had studied marketing history, it would have learned from the Schlitz Brewing Co. that it's unwise to tinker with a well-known and successful formula.

In the early 1970s, Schlitz was the second best-selling brew in the U.S.—"the beer that made Milwaukee famous." But then blunder-headed management changed the taste and created a beer that made Schlitz infamous.

In a cost-saving move in 1974, management decided to radically shorten the brewing process. Schlitz substituted cheap corn syrup for some of the costly barley malt and rushed batches through in half the time that most brewers spent. The patented brewing process, called Automated Balanced Fermentation, not only ruined the taste but left visible flakes of yeast floating in the beer. To make matters worse, drinkers couldn't find a head on their draft. Entire markets were lost virtually overnight. Sales nose-dived from 24 million barrels to 15 million in 1980. Schlitz reverted to something close to the original taste, but by then it was too late. By 1985 the brand had only 1 percent of the market.

Who's Minding the Store?

1984 growth in sales for Decision Data Computer Corp.:

1985 growth in sales for same company after 75 of its 160 salespeople topped their quotas and management rewarded them all with one-week trips to Hong Kong *at the same time* in March 1985:

The Corporate Culture That Turned Into the Corporate Cult

PROLOGUE

ComputerLand Corp. was one of the hottest franchise start-ups in the history of American enterprise. It doubled in size every year during its first seven years, as sales soared to $770 million in fiscal 1983. But within two years it nearly collapsed, partly because it's corporate culture turned into a corporate cult.

CHAPTER 1
Bill Millard starts up IMS Associates Inc., a small computer consulting and engineering firm, in 1972. He meets Werner Erhard, a former used car salesman who had changed his name from Jack Rosenberg. Erhard gains fame as founder of Erhard Seminars Training, or est, a bizarre method of consciousness-raising. New trainees undergo brutal weekends in chilled rooms, with little food, drink, rest, or bathroom breaks, to jolt them into new life perspectives.

CHAPTER 2
Millard becomes consumed by est and spends many hours teaching his employees how to "go to the center of their fears." He demands that his executives "take the training." Employees attend est seminars together where they are verbally abused in the name of "stripping them of unneeded psychological baggage."

CHAPTER 3
Millard founds ComputerLand Corp. in 1976 and tries to make everyone in the company take the training. He contracts with an Erhard organization to give an est communications seminar for his managers. He hires former est leaders and trainers and places them in important positions within the company.

CHAPTER 4
Under Millard's est-style management, the company's vice-presidents and divisional heads have no real authority. No one can make any decisions without calling two or three other people and voting on it. The officers are reduced to playing internal politics and building up their own private fiefdoms.

CHAPTER 5
ComputerLand does not react quickly or smartly enough to rapid changes in the marketplace in 1984. Service to the franchisees deteriorates as est-practicing managers answer complaints with, "Thank you for sharing that with us." By July 1985, ComputerLand is in debt to bankers and suppliers and cash is tight. While the franchisees threaten mutiny, a competitor wins a $141 million damage award against Millard and ComputerLand.

CHAPTER 6
To stave off the total collapse of the company, Millard gives up his title and his seat on the board of directors. He passes day-to-day control to a former associate and, on a court order, hands over 20 percent of the company stock, much of it to a competitor. The company goes public and is put in the hands of investors, franchisees, and its top employees—most of whom haven't taken the training.

EPILOGUE
After attracting hundreds of thousands of people to his programs and providing Millard with the philosophy that guided ComputerLand, Erhard suspends all est training everywhere.

THE UNBALANCED SHEET

BIG MONEY LOSERS

Hi-Ho Silver ... Away!

When the billionaire Hunt brothers of Texas tried to corner the silver market, they planned to line their already-bulging pockets with a few billion dollars more. Instead, they wound up getting their pockets picked.

Nelson Bunker Hunt (see photo p. 15, right) and his brothers Lamar (left) and W. Herbert accumulated some 200 million ounces of the precious metal in a daring scheme that drove silver prices from $11 per ounce in 1979 to $50 per ounce in January 1980.

But then the market collapsed—and with it went billions of dollars of the family fortune.

By 1985, the net worth of the Hunt empire was $2.2 billion—an incredible plunge from the $5.1 billion in combined wealth that they enjoyed before their silver play. The brothers' personal holdings, listed at more than $3 billion in 1980, stood at $600 million in August 1985.

To keep from going bankrupt, the brothers had to mortgage most of their personal possessions. According to biographer Harry Hurt III, author of *Texas Rich,* much of the family's shrunken treasures were put into hock, including "thousands of ancient coins from the third century B.C.; sixteenth-century antiques; Greek and Roman statuettes of bronze and silver; paintings of famous American landscape painters; fine porcelain birds; 500 racehorses with names like Overdrawn, Extravagant, and Trillionaire; over 4 million acres of oil and gas leases; over 70,000 head of cattle; even lawn mowers, CB radios, water coolers, a Rolex watch, and a Mercedes-Benz automobile."

By 1985, the Hunts had sold off 90 percent of their remaining silver hoard at a staggering loss. Mused Nelson Bunker Hunt: "A billion dollars isn't what it used to be."

Down and Out in Africa

What was the only business failure ever suffered by the late Charles Engelhard, gold tycoon and president of Engelhard Minerals & Chemicals Corp.?

Engelhard invested in an African timber estate on the banks of the Zambesi River. Not until too late did he learn that in the dry season the river reverses direction and flows inland, making it impossible to float timber to port. He tried to recoup his losses by planting crops on the estate. It would have worked—if only the Zambesi's hippopotamuses hadn't lumbered out of the river and eaten all of Engelhard's crops.

Past Winners of the "Biggest Money-Loser of the Year" Award

YEAR	COMPANY	LOSSES IN MILLIONS
1986	LTV	$3,251.6
1985	LTV	723.9
1984	A. H. Robins	461.6
1983	U.S. Steel	1,161.0
1982	International Harvester	1,638.2
1981	Ford	1,060.1
1980	Chrysler	1,709.7
1979	Chrysler	1,097.3
1978	Chrysler	204.6
1977	Bethlehem Steel	448.2
1976	Rohr Industries	52.1
1975	Singer	451.9
1974	Chrysler	52.1
1973	Genesco	52.9
1972	Boise Cascade	170.6
1971	Anaconda	356.4
1970	Northwest Industries	227.4
1969	Ling-Temco-Vought (now LTV)	38.3
1968	Celanese	77.1
1967	American Motors	75.8
1966	Douglas Aircraft	27.6
1965	Brunswick	76.9
1964	Curtis Publishing	13.9
1963	Studebaker	80.9
1962	Fairbanks Whitney	27.0
1961	General Dynamics	113.2
1960	Lockheed Aircraft	42.9
1959	Douglas Aircraft	33.8
1958	Chrysler	33.8
1957	American Motors	11.8

Breaking the Bank

*The Ten Largest Commercial Bank Failures
and Federal Bailouts (By Deposit Size)*

NAME	YEAR	ASSETS (millions)	FDIC OUTLAY (millions)
1. Continental Illinois National Bank,** Chicago	1984	33,600	4,500
2. First Pennsylvania Bank,** Philadelphia	1980	5,500	325
3. Franklin National Bank,* New York	1974	3,700	1,800
4. The First National Bank* and Trust of Oklahoma City	1986	1,600	635
5. First National Bank of Midland,* Midland, Texas	1983	1,400	1,200
6. BancTEXAS Group,** Dallas (11 banks)	1987	1,300	150
7. United States National* Bank, San Diego	1973	1,300	222
8. United American Bank,* Knoxville, Tennessee	1983	800	466
9. Banco Credito y Ahorro* Ponceno, Puerto Rico	1978	700	98
10. Park Bank of Florida,* St. Petersburg	1986	600	211

*Bank failure
**Bailout

Source: Federal Deposit Insurance Corp.

Opportunity Knocked and No One Answered

DECCA RECORDING CO.

When the Beatles auditioned for Decca in 1962, the record execs refused to sign the group because they didn't like their sound. Decca bigwig Dick Rose told Beatles' manager Brian Epstein, "Groups with guitars are on their way out." The foursome's manager begged Decca to reconsider and promised he would personally buy 3,000 copies of any single his group recorded. Decca turned a deaf ear to the Beatles. The group went with EMI . . . and the rest is history.

REMINGTON ARMS CO.

In 1897, the Wagner Typewriting Machine Co. offered to sell the patent to the typewriter to Remington Arms Co. But Remington shot down the idea of buying the patent because, its president said, "No mere machine can replace a reliable and honest clerk." Wagner was soon acquired by Underwood which went on to sell more than 12 million typewriters during the next fifty years.

WESTERN UNION TELEGRAPH CO.

When Alexander Graham Bell invented the telephone in 1876, it did not ring the bells of potential investors. His company, the Bell Telephone Co., was so desperate for cash that it offered to sell all the patents to the telephone to Western Union for $100,000. But Western Union said it had no use for "an electrical toy." Several years later, Western Union changed its mind and bought another inventor's patents for a similar device. Bell's company sued for patent infringement and won a settlement that froze Western Union out of the telephone business.

HEWLETT-PACKARD CO.

In 1975, a low-level Hewlett-Packard engineer named Steve Wozniak shared a dream with his pal Steven Jobs—to build and sell a personal computer for the masses. The pair tinkered together on their own time to create a compact PC. Their invention was offered to Hewlett-Packard, which turned thumbs down on the idea. So Wozniak and Jobs went off on their own, founded Apple Computer Inc., and helped revolutionize the personal computer industry.

DU PONT CORP.

After creating Corfam, a substitute for leather, Du Pont couldn't market it successfully in the 1960s. Corfam was put on expensive shoes to enhance its image, but sales remained sluggish—even after cheaper shoes were made of the product. Du Pont was convinced the artificial material was all but useless and sold it to Poland at a multimillion-dollar loss in 1974. Only then did the price of leather on the world market soar, making Corfam an extremely profitable material.

Melts in Your Mouth, Not in E.T.'s Hands

What company felt like choking on its own candy after it chose not to allow its product to be used in the film *E.T.*?

WHILE YOU WERE OUT

TO: E.T.
☐ URGENT   TIME: ___ A.M./P.M.
DATE: ___
FROM: M+M/MARS
OF: ___
PHONE: AREA CODE / NUMBER / EXTENSION

TELEPHONED	☒ PLEASE CALL
CAME TO SEE YOU	WANTS TO SEE YOU
RETURNED YOUR CALL	WILL CALL AGAIN

MESSAGE: We don't think it's in our best interests to use M+M's in a scene in your movie

SIGNED: ___

M&M/Mars. The company decided that nothing would be gained by allowing M&M's to appear in the movie. So Elliot wound up luring the lovable alien with Hershey's Reece's Pieces—and the memorable scene wound up luring millions of people into the stores to buy Reece's Pieces. Thanks to the megahit, Hershey's sales shot up 65 percent.

PRODUCTS OF A WARPED IMAGINATION

IDEAS THAT SHOULD HAVE BEEN KILLED BUT WEREN'T

They're New! They're Improved! ... They're Flops!
New Products That Failed

HEUBLEIN INC.
In the mid-1970s, Heublein introduced "Wine and Dine Dinner," an upscale packaged meal containing an entrée and a little bottle of wine. The wine wasn't Chateau Lafite; it was more like swill. Actually, it was a spiced and salted cooking wine that buyers were supposed to mix with the entrée. However, too many consumers didn't read the directions. They chugged the wine straight, hated it, and never bought Wine and Dine again.

GERBER PRODUCTS CO.

In the early 1970s, Gerber guessed correctly that busy young adults would be attracted to foods that could be prepared in a hurry. Trading on its success with infants, the company offered such grown-up fare as beef burgundy and Mediterranean vegetables. But Gerber made the fatal error of packaging the food in containers that looked like baby-food jars. Adults didn't want to go back to their infancy. Gerber compounded the problem by labeling the product "Singles." Single adults, already grumpy about eating alone, didn't want to be reminded of their marital status.

Gerber refused to give up and tried the teen market with "Gerber Desserts" in 1981. It ran ads in teen magazines saying, "The secret's out. Gerber isn't just for babies!" But teens refused to bite. In effect, they told market researchers, "You're crazy if you think we're going to eat baby food."

GENERAL FOODS

In 1956, General Foods created a premium food line called "Gourmet Foods" for the upscale market. The company bypassed supermarkets for select department stores, such as Lord & Taylor and Neiman-Marcus. It advertised in high-brow magazines and ignored general-interest publications. However, for every customer spreading Gourmet Foods lingonberry preserves on English muffins, there were dozens of Americans eating doughnuts and corn flakes. Before it died four years later, Gourmet Foods cost the giant company $30 million. General Foods chairman Edward Mortimer said he knew instantly why it flopped: "The wife of some fancy businessman sat next to me at a party and said, 'Oh, Mr. Mortimer, your Gourmet Foods are wonderful. We stock the yacht with them.' I thought to myself, 'Yeah, that's what's wrong—not enough yachts.'"

> What was the biggest flop for Charles Revson, president of Revlon?
> A male genitalia deodorant called Private.

AMERICAN KITCHEN FOODS INC.

In the early 1970s, Frank Aldridge, president of the french fry company, thought he had come up with a terrific idea—mash vegetables up and extrude them into the shape of french fries so picky kids would eat their spinach. Soon American Kitchen was shipping to supermarkets everywhere packages of "I Hate Peas," "I Hate Beets," "I Hate Spinach," and other extruded vegetables disguised as french fries. Mothers began snatching them off the shelves. But the nation's kids saw instantly that peas by any other shape still tasted the same. They refused to touch them with a ten-foot fork.

The Soft Drink That Exploded on the Market

It had all the ingredients of success: investors willing to put up the necessary millions, two marketing geniuses to run the company, and a soft drink containing fruit juice that appealed to Perrier buyers who wanted more flavor.

Called Napa Natural, the beverage was billed as the "world's first natural soft drink"—a can't-miss product that did miss because of one little oversight.

In 1983, the Adams Natural Beverage Co. was founded in Napa Valley, California. With investors putting up $8 million in capital, the company hired Bruce Nevins and Jim Stevens—the marketing whizzes who made Perrier a household word—to run the business.

Nevins and Stevens hired a consultant to formulate the drink, reached agreement with a Sacramento bottling plant, retained an advertising agency, and plotted the distribution strategy. The plan was to launch Napa Natural on the West Coast and then roll it out nationally.

After a year of careful planning, four flavors of Napa Natural—each containing 67 percent fruit juice and no preservatives—debuted to tremendous consumer acceptance. By the summer of 1984, Napa broke Perrier's sales record for the first six months.

Nevins, Stevens, and the Adams Natural Beverage Co. were enjoying the sweet taste of success. Then life soured.

Napa Natural cans began to explode on the store shelves! In September, stores began reporting that the cans were bulging ominously and, in some instances, blowing their lids off. It was then the company realized its oversight—it had neglected to consider that the beverage would ferment because of the high juice content. Fermentation eventually caused the cans to explode.

The company was forced to recall thousands of cases of Napa Natural. It didn't ship any cases for the next two months while the product was reformulated and the juice content reduced to 51 percent. (It was eventually lowered to 30 percent.) Unfortunately, when shipments finally resumed, some of the supermarket chains refused to take the product back. Sales of the soft drink that exploded on the market soon fizzled.

Bombs Away!

RCA CORP.

SelectaVision VideoDisc player: It took fifteen years to develop and only three years to die. Introduced in 1981, the machine played only prerecorded discs and was unable to record TV programs. RCA management totally misread consumers' fondness for videocassette recorders that play movies and other programs as well as record from television. *Loss:* $580 million

GENERAL DYNAMICS

Convair intermediate-range jet transport: The company grossly miscalculated the costs and the market for the Convair 880 and 990. Even though division heads knew they were building an expensive plane that had few advance orders, they forged ahead. Engineering snafus and cost overruns went unchecked until 1961 when the board of directors discovered that the aviation boondoggle was crippling the company. They finally grounded the project. *Loss:* $425 million

TIME INC.

TV-Cable Week and *Picture Week:* Hailed as the company's most ambitious new venture ever, *TV-Cable Week* folded after five months. The magazine, launched in 1983 to compete against *TV Guide,* published editions customized to individual cable-TV systems. But it became so expensive and labor-intensive that costs soared far beyond projections. Three years later, Time Inc. toyed around with another publication, *Picture Week.* But after an on-again, off-again publishing schedule, the ill-fated magazine was scrapped after Time had spent $40 million. *Losses:* $100 million

IBM

PCjr: In November 1983, IBM poured $40 million into the promotion of a new personal computer aimed at the home market. But PCjr missed the Christmas season on its first year because of production delays. It didn't much matter. Consumers were turned off by the machine's limited memory, Chiclet-shaped keyboard, and hefty price tag ($1,200 without the monitor). Production ceased in the spring of 1985. *Loss:* $100 million (estimated)

KNIGHT-RIDDER NEWSPAPERS

Viewtron: The computer-based home information service was launched in October 1983 because Knight-Ridder wanted to be in the vanguard should technological advances erode the newspaper business. But by 1986, the company made the bittersweet discovery that videotext was no threat to newspaper advertising or readership. The general public was not interested in paying for a technologically elaborate home information service. *Loss:* $50 million

Edsel (éd-sel) n:
Cadillac of Mistakes

If ever an automaker introduced the wrong car to the wrong market at the wrong time, it was Ford Motor Co. For thirty years, Ford has had to live with the indignity of being responsible for America's most infamous manufacturing disaster—the Edsel.

The Edsel was advertised and promoted as the people's choice after nationwide surveys were conducted to determine exactly what Americans wanted in a new car. Ford executives sifted through reams of market research—and ignored most of it. Instead, they built a car by committee. More than 4,000 executive decisions were made on everything from the shape of the door handle to the amount of chrome on the bumpers.

Sixteen thousand names were proposed for the Edsel and all were rejected—even those suggested by poet Marianne Moore, whom Ford had hired to help name the car. It was easy to understand why Ford declined her choices, which included "Intelligent Bullet," "Utopian Turtletop," and "Mongoose Civique." Eventually, the Ford family decided to name the car in memory of Edsel Ford, the only son of founder Henry Ford. It turned out to be a hell of a way to honor someone.

When the car was introduced in the fall of 1957, people kept talking about its toilet-seat-shaped grille; its widespread, winged rear end; and its push-button gear selector on the hub of the steering wheel. To Ford's dismay, that's all people did—talk, not buy. Unfortunately, the Edsel was introduced when America was hit with the worst recession at that time since the Great Depression. The Edsel was also plagued with power-steering and cooling-system problems, oil leaks, and stuck hoods and trunks.

So few Edsels were bought that Ford lost about $3,000 on each car. After taking a two-year, $350 million bath, Ford sent the Edsel to the scrap heap. According to estimates, it would have been cheaper for Ford to have given away a new Mercury to every Edsel buyer instead of selling them an Edsel.

Why did Simmons & Co., the mattress manufacturer, fail so miserably in Japan in the 1960s despite a major sales campaign?

The Japanese have traditionally slept on floor mats.

Maybe We Should Have Done More Market Research

Companies Whose Products Didn't Trigger a Run on the Grocery Stores

MLO Products: Gorilla Balls protein supplement snack
Quaker Bonnet: Buffalo Chip chocolate cookies
To-Fitness Inc.: To-Fitness Tofu Pasta
Health Valley Natural Foods: Parsnip Chips
Jac Creative Foods: Sea Lion seafood bologna and Sea Lami seafood salami
Reese Finer Foods Valley Corp: Norwoods Egg Coffee
Beverage Capital Corp: Moon Shine "sippin' citrus"
Clairol: A Touch of Yogurt shampoo
Helene Curtis: Gimme Cucumber hair conditioner
Jheri Redding Products: Chocolate Styling Gel
International Yogurt Co.: Yogurt Face & Body Powder, "containing a large amount of living yogurt culture"

CAPITALIZING CAPITALISTS

MAKING MONEY THE OLD-FASHIONED WAY
—by Exploitation

Laying in Weight

In November 1985, floods ravaged West Virginia, causing millions of dollars in damage and forcing thousands to flee their homes.

It was a trying time for the people of the Mountaineer State. But Weight Watchers thought it was the perfect time to nag people about their weight.

While flood waters were still cresting in some towns, Weight Watchers—a division of H. J. Heinz Co.—had the audacity to issue a press release designed to drum up business among the water-logged citizenry. "Don't let this flood be fattening," advised Millie Snyder, Weight Watchers' West Virginia area director. People were advised to "stay afloat" emotionally and not "sink into despair" by compulsive overeating.

"As we see our possessions float away and homes ruined, it's easy to throw up our hands and say, 'Why bother?'" said the release. "After everything finally dries out and the mess is cleaned up, we'll then have extra pounds to cope with."

When *The Wall Street Journal* asked Weight Watchers if there were any second thoughts about the press release, a spokeswoman said no. "Hard experience tells us that any kind of excuse like this is reason for people to gain weight."

Anything for a Buck

Bloomingdale's in New York opened a "Street Couture" boutique in 1983 featuring clothes that were ragged, tattered, and spattered. A spokesman said, "Bag ladies are in and so is the 'street look.'"

Rage Music International Inc. marketed *The American Gun Album: A Celebration in Song*. Among the original country music selections: "Thank You, Smith & Wesson," "America Was Born with a Gun in Her Hand," "Never Mind the Dog, Beware of the Owner," and "Gun Totin' Woman."

Pepperidge Farm, of Clinton, Connecticut, came up with a holiday gift selection in 1980 for those who believe in killing 'em with kindness—individually wrapped chocolate praline-filled shotgun shells.

Paperback Games, of Bethesda, Maryland, created "The Subway Vigilante Game." A description of the game in its catalog reads: "Fed up with punks that terrorize the urban landscape? Now you can fight back in the comfort of your own home with 'The Subway Vigilante Game.' That's right! Each player starts out on the streets of Brooklyn with a 'gun' token and six 'bullets.' The object is to get home to the Bronx alive. On your way, you'll encounter the vermin of the city. Run out of bullets and you're mugged! Comes with four tokens—die-cast metal miniatures of snub-nosed .38, .357 Magnum, .380 automatic, and .45 automatic—plus twenty-four bullets, paper playing board, 'Make My Day' cards, and complete instructions."

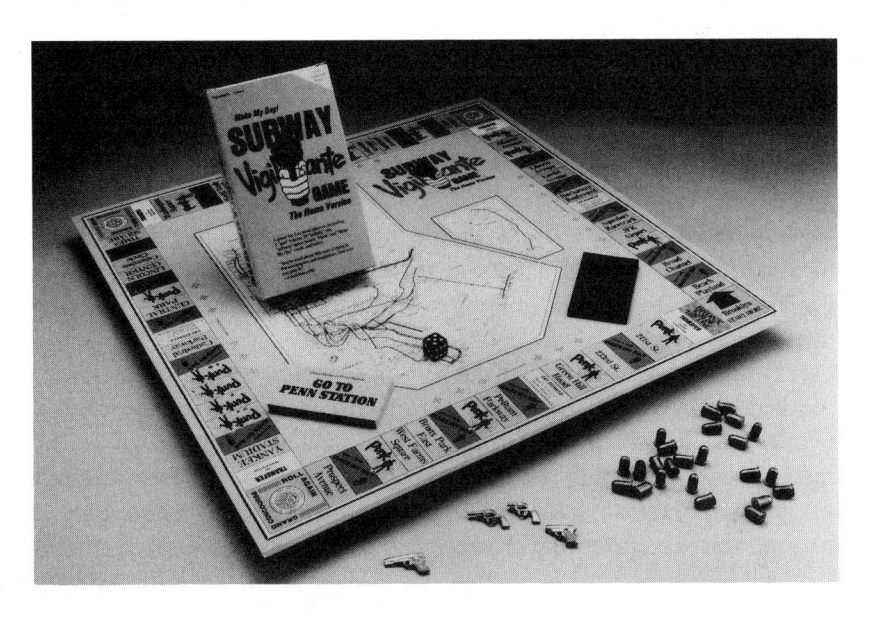

A Tailor-Made Layoff

When Eastman Kodak Co. announced plans in February 1986 to cut its work force by 10 percent, a men's clothing store in the company's home town of Rochester, New York, took the news as a golden opportunity to drum up business.

Ostensibly to rally behind the soon-to-be unemployed, The Clothing Center placed an ad in the local newspaper that said, "Any economic problem Rochester may face is our problem [or in this case, opportunity] as well." Noting that hundreds of Kodak employees would be looking for work, the ad said, "Nothing is more important in finding a new job than the proper executive dress." The store offered 25 percent discounts for "all Rochester men."

Sales boomed. But there was at least one businessman annoyed with the ad—Robert Bussell, who just happened to own The Clothing Center. "I considered the thing in poor taste," he said. Bussell said he was away on a cruise and got back too late to cancel the ad, which was conceived and placed by the store's ad agency, Scheer Advertising Agency of New Jersey.

Lynch Mob

As a member of the aggressive sales force of Merrill Lynch & Co., a young account executive decided to prey upon the misfortune of several thousand people who lost their money when a local thrift institution collapsed.

In September 1984, the Merrill Lynch salesman showed up at a Danville, California, meeting of 2,500 angry depositors of Western Community MoneyCenter, a savings and loan association that failed several months earlier. The depositors had yet to get any of their money back.

The salesman set up a card table in the high school gym where the meeting was being held and tried to sell them a secure mutual fund. He thought a government-guaranteed investment would sound good to them.

It didn't. "I couldn't believe someone could be so cold-blooded," recalled Bill Sullivan, an organizer of the meeting. "Some of our people had lost their life savings." Sullivan lost his patience at the meeting and personally ejected the Merrill Lynch representative. A company spokesman had a slightly different version: "The salesman realized this was an unruly crowd so he left."

CHIEF EGOMANIACS AND OPPRESSORS (CEOs)

The J. R. Ewing Award

CHARLES REVSON
President of Revlon (1958–75)
Ruthless, crude, arbitrary whip-cracker who deliberately made employees paranoid ... "He chewed up executives the way some people chew vitamins," said a former exec ... Hired and fired receptionists to go with changing decor of his offices, humiliated employees with obscene verbal assaults, and pretended to sleep during presentations ... Would carry Christmas bonus checks of execs in his pocket for months, then say, "Here, kiddie, here's a check for you." (left)

ROBERT ABBOUD
Chairman and CEO of First Chicago Corp. (1975–80)
Called "Idi" (after Ugandan dictator Idi Amin) by staff behind his back ... Berated senior executives in front of their own subordinates ... Had the habit of ignoring and belittling his brain trust and refused to delegate much authority ... Created an aura of wealth and power and reminded underlings that it all came from him ... When he was fired, employees sang, "Ding-dong, the witch is gone." (right)

ROBERT MALOTT
Chairman of FMC Corp. (1972–present)
A master of confrontation who conducts meetings with a verbal cattle prod ... Grills subordinates mercilessly and abusively for no good reason ... Often shows boredom during meetings by reading mail or leaving room in middle of presentation ... Said one exec: "We play a semi-Machiavellian game just to function with him. We spend an unconscionable amount of time trying to find out when he'll be least obnoxious." (left, p. 35)

RICHARD JACOB
Chairman and CEO of Day International (1971–present)
Known as "Old Rough-Tough" because he conducts business the same way he did in days as World War II warrant officer . . . Sharp-tongued and brutal to those who don't go along with his ideas . . . Once threatened to kick security analyst in the groin for interrupting him . . . "Do something wrong and he lands on you, all 300 pounds," said an exec . . . When disappointed over performance of two managers, he pinned their bonus checks to his desk in full view for all to see for months before handing over the money. (right)

FRED ACKMAN
Chairman of Superior Oil Co. (1981–84)
An autocratic ruler with a Napoleon complex who even refused to discuss staff suggestions . . . Treated execs' disagreement with him as disloyalty . . . Said former staffer: "He couldn't stand it when somebody disagreed with him, even in private. He'd eat you alive, calling you a dumb SOB or asking if you had your head up your ass" . . . Abusive temper, short stature, and red hair earned him behind-the-back nickname of "Little Red Fred" . . . Nine of thirteen top executives quit within a year after he took over. (not pictured)

What did an executive who worked under Thomas Mellon Evans, chairman and CEO of Crane Co.—and considered one of corporate America's toughest bosses in 1980—say to a fifty-year-old manager who was considering accepting a job with Evans?

"If you want to see fifty-five, I'd think twice about it."

MAURICE "HANK" GREENBERG
President and CEO of American International Group Inc. (1967–present) An unrelenting, demanding ruler who believes the company comes above all else ... Doesn't hesitate to call subordinates in the middle of the night and give them orders ... Said one exec: "He pays little attention to time zones, so he is always calling people at home ... The people who report to Hank are put under pressure that could be considered unreal" ... Accomplished at belittling employees in front of others ... "You haven't achieved any standing if you haven't experienced his wrath," said a staffer who had.

Words to Work By

Robert Malott, chairman of FMC Corp., on running a corporation, 1980:

"Leadership is demonstrated when the ability to inflict pain is confirmed."

J. E. Davis, president of the Winn-Dixie grocery chain, extolling the virtues of unemployment in his company's house organ, 1980:

"We cannot run good stores when unemployment by government standards is below 5 percent ... Productivity even for you and me is better when two or three people are waiting at the door for our jobs."

D. J. Sullivan, southern district manager for Roadway Express, in a memo to supervisors:

"Gentlemen, I'm tired of requesting, I'm tired of trying to show you the importance of taking on labor. It sure appears that many of you don't have the balls you were born with ... I want more suspensions. And I want more discharges. I want them now and I want them every period from now on."

Charles Revson, president of Revlon, after changing advertising agencies seven times in three years, 1963:
"Creative people are like a wet towel. You wring them out and pick up another one."

Wallace Rasmussen, chairman of Beatrice Foods, in answer to a colleague's question about how to handle the family during one's climb up the corporate ladder:
"Get rid of them if they get in the way."

Legends in Their Own Minds

ARMAND HAMMER
Chairman of Occidental Petroleum (1957–present)
Commissioned and subsidized the 1985 publishing of a lavish book called *The World of Armand Hammer,* consisting of 255 oversized pages of color photographs of himself, his associates, and his possessions ... Included in the book was a two-page photo of himself in bed, simultaneously—according to the caption—watching four TVs, eating breakfast, reading the paper, and "arranging by phone to have tea with the visiting Deputy Prime Minister of Bulgaria."

RICHARD ROSENTHAL
Chairman of Citizens Utilities Co. (1946–81)
Has been called an incredible egomaniac by own staff ... When flying on commercial airlines, has been known to give a letter to pilot instructing him how to take off and land ... Set a record when he ran forty-eight photographs of himself in company's 1980 annual report ... Took up sixteen pages of 1984 AR's fifty-two pages detailing his accomplishments in acting, teaching, business, and other pursuits ... Says one associate: "Richard is an intellectual tyrant and I resent the need to constantly feed his ego."

DONALD TRUMP
President of the Trump Organization (1979–present)
Has ego as big as his giant buildings ... Attaches name to most every building he buys or builds—except for subsidized housing projects ... Sued Eddie and Julius Trump of the Trump Group because he claimed they were trying to cash in on his name. Never mind that they had been using it in their business for twenty years—long before he hit the big time. Was unsuccessful in lawsuit.

HARRY E. FIGGIE, JR.
President of Figgie International Holdings (1963–present)
Used company's annual reports for personal pontificating ... In the 1982 AR, he gave shareholders a thirteen-page personal perspective on the recessionary period ... Wrote a twenty-page recollection of his business life in 1983 AR ... Penned another essay on the "problems facing the industry today" for the 1985 AR ... Now offers reprints of what he calls his "trilogy."

JAMES DUTT
Chairman and CEO of Beatrice Companies Inc. (1979–85)
Had large photos of himself put up in lobbies of every one of company's offices and factories ... Was given nickname "Chairman Dutt" by employees because photos reminded them of Chairman Mao's pictures hanging everywhere in China.

CONRAD BLACK
Chairman of Argus Ltd. (1979–present)
Commissioned four-foot-high portrait of himself in full-dress uniform of Napoleon Bonaparte, complete with medals and sash and right hand tucked into vest.

What did Willard Butcher, chairman of Chase Manhattan Bank, tell guests at a shrimp-and-champagne reception in 1981 was the best way he had found to solicit opinions of ordinary folks about President Reagan's economic programs?

Once in a while, he said, instead of riding around New York City in his chauffeured limousine, he took a taxi to listen to what the cabbie had to say.

LOOKING OUT FOR NO. 1

HIGH PAY FOR LOW RETURN

If Only He Practiced What He Preached

In speeches during 1984 and 1985, T. Boone Pickens assailed companies that didn't share their huge cash flows with stockholders.

However, he failed to tell his audiences that his own Mesa Petroleum Co. had fattened his wallet considerably while ignoring its shareholders.

As Mesa's chairman, Pickens became the highest-paid executive of any public company in 1984, earning a whopping $22.8 million. Yet Mesa's dividend payout for the year totaled only $14 million. In fact, from 1981 to 1984, during which Mesa garnered $1 billion in greenmail profit, the company neither upped its meager dividend nor bought back its stock to split the booty with shareholders.

For a self-proclaimed defender of the stockholder, Pickens was mighty silent in November 1984 when Mesa's board of directors created the Deferred Bonus and Incentive Award Plans to "retain, reward, and properly motivate key employees." The board set aside $20 million as a reward for Mesa's $404 million pretax greenmail profit in its takeover battle for Gulf Oil.

Almost all the bonus money went to Pickens. The chairman, who already received a salary and bonus of $4.2 million in 1984, was given an additional $18.6 million in "deferred compensation units" that he personally could use to play along with Mesa in future takeover attempts. Mesa's board also made Pickens a gift of another $7.6 million in "loan" chits for speculating—at no risk—on future deals. This allowed him to earn $5.5 million, or 6.9 percent of Mesa's profits, in a raid on Phillips Petroleum.

Even though Mesa posted a 34.2 percent return on equity in 1984, it yielded only a 7 percent return to shareholders over the previous three years. Meanwhile, Pickens—the so-called champion of the American stockholder—was named by *Business Week* as the CEO who produced the lowest profits and shareholder gains for his pay in 1984.

Parachuting into the Land of the Super Rich

When Pantry Pride took over Revlon Inc. in 1985, Michel Bergerac, chairman of the giant health and beauty company, pulled the ripcord on the largest golden parachute ever—a whopping $35 million.

As part of Bergerac's original contract with Revlon in 1974, the company offered him a severance package that included five years of salary and bonuses, valued at nearly $7 million, and stock options worth $13 million. Then, in 1983, the Revlon board added another $15 million to his golden parachute so he wouldn't pass up a good takeover deal for fear of losing his job.

Said a Revlon director, "If a buyer came along, we wanted him [Bergerac] to do what was best for the stockholders." Apparently, the director failed to realize that Bergerac was already getting paid a hefty salary to do what was best for the stockholders.

Under Bergerac, Revlon's revenues quadrupled to $2 billion. However, its earnings had fallen from a peak of $192 million in 1980 to $125 million in 1985 when Bergerac opened his $35 million parachute

"HOORAY! I'VE BEEN KICKED OUT BY THE BOARD!"

following the Pantry Pride takeover. "Clearly, it's an enormous amount of money," he told *Business Week*. "Whether it should be less or more, how do you judge those things? I don't know." Nevertheless, he said, he was "delighted to abide by the wisdom of the board."

Happy Landings!

The Ten Largest Golden Parachutes in 1986

	COMPANY	WHAT LED TO PAYMENT	TOTAL PACKAGE* THOUSANDS OF DOLLARS
1. Thomas M. Macioce, Chmn.	Allied Dept. Stores	Campeau takeover	$13600
2. Thomas H. Wyman, Chmn.	CBS	Ousted by board	11439
3. Gerald S. Office, Jr., Chmn.	Ponderosa	Asher Edelman takeover	8300
4. Gerald G. Probst, CEO	Sperry	Burroughs merger	6670
5. Michel Vaillaud, Chmn.	Schlumberger	Ousted by board	6200
6. John R. Miller, Pres.	Standard Oil	Resigned under pressure	5623
7. Joseph H. Johnson, Chmn.	Assoc. Dry Goods	May Dept. Stores takeover	4900
8. Anthony Luiso, Exec. V-P	Beatrice	Leveraged buyout	4557
9. John D. Macomber, Chmn.	Celanese	Hoechst takeover	4514
10. Ralph P. Davidson, Chmn.**	Time	Early retirement	4029

DATA: COMPANY REPORTS, BUSINESS WEEK ESTIMATES

*Includes final salary, bonus, long-term compensation, certain retirement benefits, and estimated future annuity payments as well as parachute **Executive committee

Reprinted from May 5, 1986, issue of *Business Week* by special permission, © 1986 by McGraw-Hill, Inc.

Words to Live By

Ivan Boesky (left), the king of arbitrage, a year before he was fined $100 million and imprisoned for insider trading:

"I think greed is healthy. You can be greedy and still feel good about yourself."

Corporate raider James Goldsmith (right):
"Takeovers are for the public good, but that's not why I do it. I do it to make money."

Living Well at Shareholders' Expense

Things that Victor Posner, chairman of Sharon Steel Corp., considered legitimate business expenses in 1978:

- Rent on his New York living quarters at the Plaza Hotel
- His limousine and driver, along with grocery, liquor, and restaurant bills
- Limousine and driver for his daughter Gail, plus her use of a company jet and yacht
- His son Steven's vacation expenses in the Catskills and Westhampton, plus a $100,000 Stutz automobile for Steven

All $1.7 million worth of Posner's writeoff was challenged by the Securities and Exchange Commission.

What was the classic inside deal of 1986?

Kohlberg Kravis Roberts & Co.'s $45 million payment for advising itself. The firm, which specializes in arranging leveraged buyouts, was a majority partner in the $6.4 billion purchase of Beatrice Companies. To help raise the money, KKR set up BCI Holdings Corp., which in turn agreed to pay the firm that whopping advisory fee.

Just When You Thought It Was Safe to Invest in a Movie Studio

Why were stockholders at the 1978 annual meeting of MCA Inc. up in arms over the amount paid an actress for a supporting role in the company's film *Jaws II*?

MCA paid actress Lorraine Gary $242,349 for her minor part in the film when the standard fee for such work was $25,000. Perhaps MCA felt Miss Gary possessed star quality; never mind that she was the wife of Sid Sheinberg, MCA's president and chief operating officer.

Money Talks

What directors of Pacific Lumber Co. called a 1985 unsolicited takeover offer from Maxxam Group Inc.:

"Not only inadequate but unconscionable."

What Pacific's CEO Gene Elam said two weeks later after his company accepted Maxxam's 4-percent-higher offer—which guaranteed a severance package for Pacific's board and executives and two years' pay for thirty-four middle managers:

"The early harsh words were illustrative of the posturing of all takeover fights."

What Pacific's shareholders said of management's self-serving agreement:

"We're suing!" And they did.

THE BUSINESS HALL OF SHAME

CHARTER MEMBERS

They were smooth, successful businessmen who used their talents and energies in twisted ways to reap millions. With perseverance, determination, and intelligence, they often cheated innocent investors, exploited their workers, flouted federal laws, and invented devious trade practices to set the substandard for the business world. That the public questioned and protested the propriety of their ways did not trouble them a bit. America was theirs for the taking—and they grabbed as much as they could.

CORNELIUS VANDERBILT (1794–1877)

A coldhearted opportunist who would stop at nothing to destroy the competition . . . Would watch a rival build up a business and then attack him by every means possible to ruin him or buy him off . . . Threatened two steamship companies with competition, then extracted $56,000 a month from them just to stay out . . . When asked by the government to put together a transport fleet, he charged suppliers exorbitant prices for ship rentals, often double what the government had paid to charter the same ship earlier . . . Used ships that were barely seaworthy and crammed 900 soldiers onto vessels whose capacity was only 300 . . . Was punished by a Senate resolution of censure but managed to get his name expunged from the record. (left)

DANIEL DREW (1797–1879)

One of Wall Street's major stock manipulators in the 1800s . . . As a youth, he brought new meaning to the term "watered stock"—he kept his cattle thirsty until he brought them to market and let them drink their fill to make them heavier for fatter profits . . . Became officer of the Erie Railroad and manipulated its stock by "accidentally" dropping a slip of paper on the floor of the Stock Exchange. Another broker picked it up and saw that the paper was a "buy" order for Erie. Then everyone bought. Drew sold short, then dumped what he already held on the market, making a killing. (right)

CHARLES YERKES (1837-1905)

A notorious, corrupt operator who controlled mayors, governors, and legislators ... After serving a prison term for embezzlement, he secured control of Chicago's horse-car lines, electrified them, and built the "Loop," the elevated railway line that encircles downtown ... Bought off Chicago aldermen to ensure his use of the streets and reorganized his companies repeatedly while drawing in the public with watered stock ... Unloaded his holdings for $20 million, sailed to England, and was never heard from again. (left)

JAY GOULD (1836-1892)

An unscrupulous financier who relished the destruction of others ... Bold, corrupt, and amoral, a master at fleecing partners and looting the companies he controlled ... Would buy several deteriorating railroad lines, combine them under a new name, issue bonds for improvements, and then sell for an enormous profit without improving the physical assets ... Nearly cornered the gold market, then sold his hoard at a profit as the U.S. Treasury flooded the market with gold, driving prices down. Had to escape through the back door of his office from gold speculators who wanted to lynch him ... From then on, was known as "The Skunk of Wall Street." (right)

ANDREW CARNEGIE (1835–1919)

Dubbed "the arch-sneak of his age" . . . Sold millions of dollars' worth of bridge and railroad bonds that he knew were bad or worthless . . . Manipulated stock prices up and down, buying and selling to take advantage of fluctuations . . . Was party to clandestine stock deals in Union Pacific Railroad, Western Union, and Pullman Company . . . Built up the steel industry by getting maximum production of steel in the shortest possible time regardless of wear and tear on men and machinery . . . Played on workers' jealousies and rivalries to surpass each other's labor . . . Used secret rebates with railroad lines to gain edge over the competition . . . Was caught trying to gyp the navy by selling it inferior armor plating. (left)

JOHN D. ROCKEFELLER (1839–1937)

Superstar of industrial monopoly . . . As head of Standard Oil, controlled all existing pipeline systems and 80 percent of U.S. oil output through secret railroad rebates, corporate espionage, preferential rate systems, and violent goon tactics . . . Cheated a widowed mother and her orphans who had inherited an oil refinery by paying them only a third of its value . . . Forced clients of independent oil dealers to buy from Standard by threatening to open a competing business, sell goods at cost, and drive them into bankruptcy . . . Imposed unfair terms on independent oil producers through his pipelines, refusing them storage and forcing them to sell oil they drilled at depressed prices. (right)

J. PAUL GETTY (1892–1976)

Penny-pinching billionaire oil baron . . . Stooped so low that he cheated his own mother in a family business trust agreement . . . Made millions by openly flouting President Eisenhower's imposition of quotas to restrict import of foreign crude oil . . . Had obsession about cheapness and held overhead down by skimping on personnel . . . To save money, ordered change in how toilets were flushed by his workers in Middle East oil fields . . . Insisted overseas managers report to him by mail, not telephone or cable because it cost too much . . . In his last twenty-five years, he never visited headquarters of his oil empire in Los Angeles or attended a single board of directors' or annual shareholders' meeting.

DEPRECIATING THE COMPANY

TARNISHING THE CORPORATE IMAGE

Alimentary, My Dear Watson

After Houston Natural Gas Corp. merged with InterNorth Inc. in 1985, the new pipeline company decided to create a slicker image with a different name.

It hired the New York consulting firm Lippincott & Margulies, Inc., which spent about four months sifting through hundreds of names before coming up with the proposed name—Enteron Corporation.

The appellation was a little hard for shareholders to stomach—the dictionary defines the word "enteron" as "the alimentary canal," or the human digestive tract. Naming their company—which owns 37,000 miles of natural-gas pipeline—after the digestive tract left the company open to ridicule.

A company spokesman tried to soothe objections by telling the press, "The dictionary definition [of enteron] describes a very efficient pipeline which is vital to life and which provides nourishment. In a subtle sort of way, that's an accurate description."

Maybe a little too accurate for InterNorth investors who complained that Houston Natural Gas Corp. made out better in the merger. In fact, they wondered what end of the enteron they wound up with—the part that digests food or the part that eliminates waste.

The name was finally changed to Enron. The shareholders accepted the new moniker in 1986, but still suffered from acute indigestion over the company's $4.3 billion debt and its 42 percent drop in income.

What Happened When "The Great Gritzbe's Flying Food Show" Restaurant Changed Its Name To "The Not So Great Gritzbe's"

| Business before name change | Business one month after name change | Business three months after name change |

Richard Melman, president of Lettuce Entertain You Enterprises, the company that owned the Chicago restaurant for ten years, decided to change the name in 1983 when slipping profits were not so great. Said Melman: "Our name change was tremendously effective because people believed it—and stopped coming." He closed the restaurant.

Banking on the Ridiculous

Continental Illinois Bank—which suffered the biggest bank failure in history in 1984 and had to be rescued by a $4.5 billion federal government bail-out—needed a new image as a reorganized, responsible, trustworthy institution. So it came up with the slogan, "We work hard. We have to."

Potential customers were hard-pressed to believe the bank's sincerity. One of Continental's 1986 TV ads featured a bank spokesman twirling a Hula Hoop around his neck to music while an 800 number for loan applications flashed on the screen. The spokesman asked viewers to dial the number while the "stupid commercial"—his words—was on.

In other spots in the campaign, bank spokesmen appeared on the screen playing the harmonica and twirling batons.

The commercials won awards but also created an image of a troubled bank that was being run by a bunch of fun-loving goof-offs.

Sticky Business

When AT&T wanted to upgrade its image in the South, the company put its servicemen through the wringer.

In 1982, Ma Bell asked its repair people to start wearing dress shirts and ties on the job. It also gave them attaché cases for their tools, renamed them "system technicians," and provided them with unmarked cars. The new image was supposed to impress business customers.

But Ma Bell didn't install air conditioning in its cars. That was no big deal in the spring. However, during the hot, steamy summer, technicians arrived on the job looking like they had just stepped out of a sauna.

The technicians, members of the Communication Workers of America, complained that they didn't look presentable when they visited their customers. "Technicians say it's hard to have corporate appeal if their shirt is wringing wet," William Lassiter, president of the Mobile, Alabama, local complained to *The Wall Street Journal*. "People ask if they've been running."

System technicians still had to climb poles and crawl under houses, although they were allowed to change into overalls first. Those technicians who opposed the voluntary new look felt they had no choice but to go along with the change in image. "If you don't put on a tie," one technician told the *Journal,* "you wind up climbing poles more often."

Have an Ingrate Day!

When two New Yorkers returned a lost envelope containing $10 million worth of AT&T commercial paper, the megacorp had a golden opportunity to enhance its image. It could have publicly praised the men for their honesty and given them a few hundred bucks in gratitude.

Instead, all Ma Bell did was send them a brief note commending them on their "prompt and honest actions." And even then, the note came only after the men had asked AT&T for the thanks.

In July 1981, New York City Housing Authority officials Harvey Bugner and Edward Egan spotted an envelope on the sidewalk in front of the phone company's headquarters. Inside were $10 million in negotiable securities payable to the bearer. The men returned them to an AT&T official who said a messenger from the securities firm of Goldman, Sachs & Co. had accidentally dropped the envelope.

"When we gave AT&T the envelope, they said thanks and then gave us the brushoff," said Bugner. "Why, they didn't even want to take our names. They didn't display the gratitude that I'd have shown had I been on their end. What if someone else had found the notes and cashed them or thrown them away? Imagine the time and expense we saved the company in paperwork had it been forced to replace the notes.

"We didn't hear a word from AT&T until I called them. Only then did we get this brief thank-you note and that was it. About three months later, an article appeared in the business press saying the reward was suitable for framing but not for much else. After that, the brokerage firm called us in, listened to our story, and gave each of us $200. But we never heard another word from AT&T. They sure missed the boat on improving their image with the little guy."

Brand XXX

Procter & Gamble's Problem: Find the right model to convey an image of innocence, purity, and softness for Ivory Snow soap flakes in 1970.

Solution: Hire model Marilyn Briggs to pose as a Madonna-like mother holding a baby for a picture to be displayed on boxes of Ivory Snow.

Procter & Gamble's Bigger Problem: It discovers in 1973 that the sweet model pictured on the millions of Ivory Snow boxes is something less than 99 and 44/100 percent pure. She is none other than porno star Marilyn Chambers, famed for her sexploits in the XXX-rated film *Behind the Green Door.*

Damned If You Do

Mother Jones' Son's Software Corp. of Buena Park, California, made no bones about its get-tough image with customers who were thinking about unlawfully copying its software program.

Its 1984 sales agreements clearly stated that if a buyer dared to copy the program illegally, "ownership of your eternal soul passes to us, and we have the right to negotiate the sale of said soul."

Just to make sure there was no misunderstanding, the agreement further warned, "Our attorneys will see to it that life on earth, as you know it, is completely ruined."

That Killer Image

When Commonwealth Edison Co. battled a flock of starlings, the power company's image wound up as stained as a statue in a bird sanctuary.

In the winter of 1986, 300,000 starlings began roosting at ComEd's power plant in Kincaid, Illinois. The company decided to evict the unwelcome fowl because droppings were piling up at the rate of an inch a week.

ComEd tried noisemakers, stuffed owls, and shotgun fire to get rid of the birds. When all that failed, the company turned to chemical warfare—it set up Rid-a-Bird pesticide-loaded perches designed to poison the starlings on contact. Soon, thousands upon thousands of starlings dropped dead to the ground.

Outraged wildlife lovers began calling the power company ComDead because of the unexpected massacre created by the poison perches. Not only were nearly 270,000 starlings killed, but so were untold numbers of hawks, owls, cats, and dogs near the plant. Experts discovered that the birds had absorbed heavy doses of the pesticide, which in turn was passed on to other neighborhood animals that were eating the dead birds.

The power company quickly pulled down the perches. But the damage had already been done to the local wildlife and to the corporate image.

Why did shareholders at Lockheed Corp.'s 1984 annual meeting wonder if the company's high-tech image was slipping?

While chairman Roy A. Anderson was proudly explaining the company's resurgence as a high-technology leader, his slide projector went haywire. When he tried to joke about this embarrassing mishap, his microphone went dead.

ALL HYPED UP

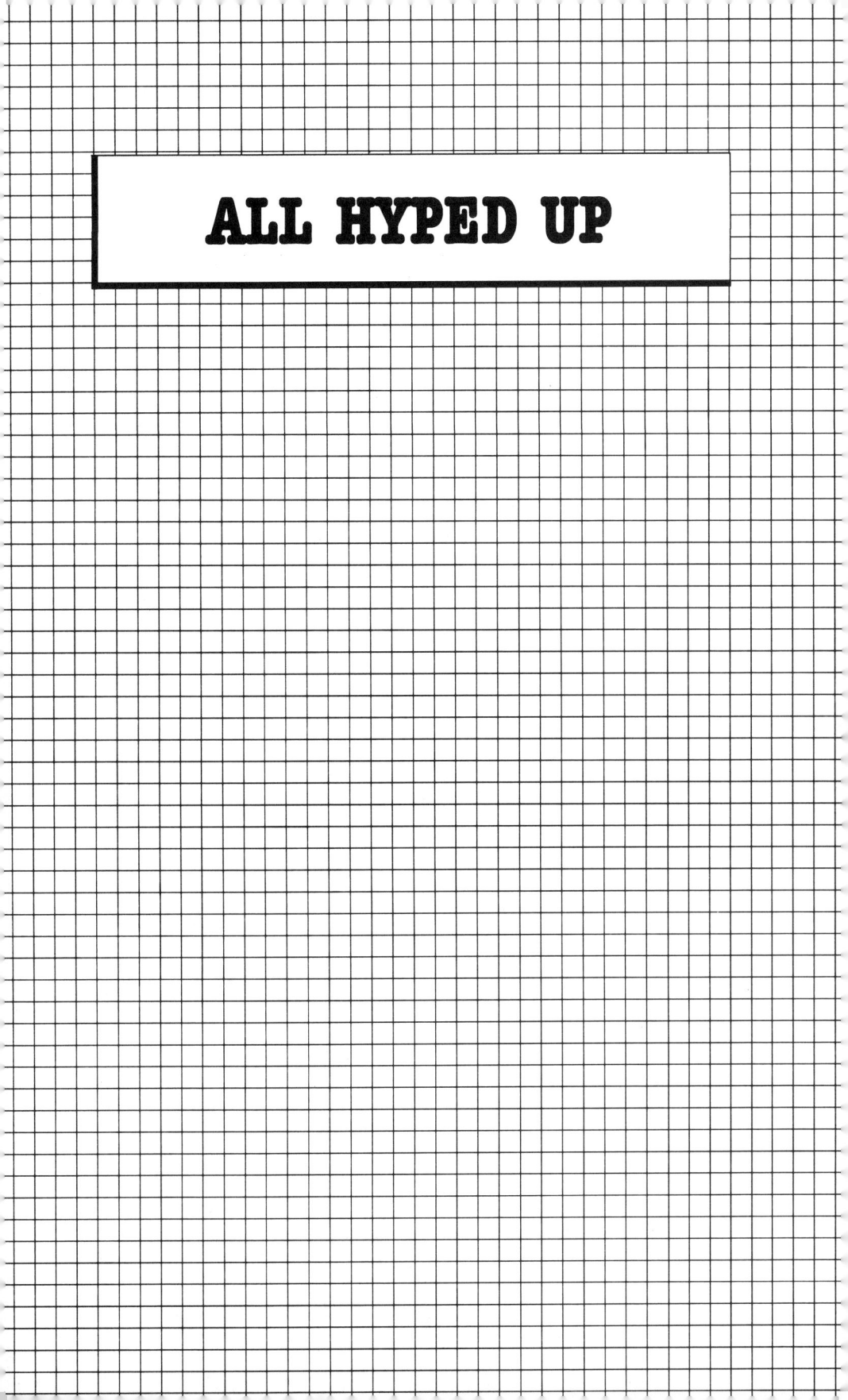

PUBLIC RELATIONS FLACKERY AND FOUL-UPS

Sugarcoating the Poison Pill

In the world of corporate communications, what looks, feels, and smells like bad news is often transformed through creative prose into a rosy picture. For example:

Herbalife International Inc. agreed to pay $850,000 in 1986 to settle charges by authorities that it made false claims in promoting its nutritional and weight-loss products.

But was the company contrite and embarrassed? No way. Here's what company president Mark Hughes had to say in a press release: "Today represents a milestone for Herbalife—a solid foundation that is built on the confidence given to us today by statements issued by state and federal regulatory agencies. I am pleased to announce that, after more than a year and a half of discussions and negotiations with the Food and Drug Administration, the California State Attorney General, and the California Department of Health, all three agencies have independently determined that Herbalife products have been and still are safe for the American public. Furthermore, all of our product claims, labeling, and marketing materials are now in conformance with the spirit and the letter of both federal and state law."

First Jersey Securities Inc. was lambasted by a scathing cover story in the July 16, 1984, issue of *Forbes* magazine that described the fast-growing brokerage business as "a marriage of greed and gullibility."

In a colossal show of chutzpah, First Jersey's PR staff twisted the article to the company's advantage—by displaying the cover of the magazine on the cover of a laudatory brochure mailed out to brokers and customers.

"First Jersey's growth has been reported by our nation's media including . . . a cover story in *Forbes* magazine," crowed the brochure, which wisely carried no text of the *Forbes* article. The brochure even included a "Letters to the Editor" column that unsuspecting readers thought was about the *Forbes* article. None of the letters were. They were in response to other, more favorable stories about First Jersey.

Republic Airlines suffered a first-quarter loss in 1981 of $15.2 million, but its PR flacks saw nothing but blue skies.

Their news release stated, "The board of directors confirmed the company's basic financial strength by declaring a cash dividend of ten cents a share." What Republic didn't say was that it used to pay twenty cents a share.

Republic's news releases often showed a flair for creativity. A release in February 1980 reported that Republic's net income for 1979 "reached" $13.1 million—but it neglected to mention that the result represented a 47 percent decline in profit and that the company had a $2.7 million loss in the fourth quarter.

Mattel reported lower earnings in 1984, but the toy company saw that as good news, not bad.

After a PR huddle, the company issued a press release that said, "The moderation in sales growth in the third quarter from the first half of the year is a measure of our success at increasing year-round demand for toys and providing greater balance to our production and shipping schedules."

Sometimes even the craftiest PR flacks can't turn bad news into good. Nevertheless, they can still soften it. For example:

Dow Chemical Corp. tried to minimize the growing concern over the threat of dioxin. In 1983, Dow spokesmen said that while it was true that dioxin was present in the environment and was highly toxic, it did not constitute a serious problem. "There is a difference between toxicity and hazard," said a Dow executive. "Just because it is a risk doesn't mean you are in danger."

The Tobacco Institute claims that smoking is not the killer the Surgeon General contends it is. "It is a habit rather than an addiction," says a spokesperson. "If tobacco were addicting, there would not be those people who have quit."

What's the Meaning of This?

Comment from a Commonwealth Edison Co. spokesman after the Nuclear Regulatory Commission found two operators asleep on the job at the Dresden nuclear plant near Chicago in 1980:

"It depends on your definition of asleep. They weren't stretched out. They had their eyes closed. They were seated at their desks with their heads in a nodding position."

Translating PR Doublespeak into Plain English

PR Doublespeak: IBM announced in 1985 that it had "completed production" of its PCjr model computer.
Plain English: IBM discontinued manufacturing its PCjr.

PR Doublespeak: The Bank of Boston said in 1985 that its failure to report $1.22 billion in cash transfers with foreign banks was merely a "systems failure," an "internal administrative glitch."
Plain English: The bank pleaded guilty to a felony charge of knowingly and willfully failing to report cash transfers.

PR Doublespeak: McDonald's Corporation announced in 1986 that it was revealing the ingredients of its fast food due to "increasing consumer interest."
Plain English: McDonald's agreed to provide the information only after pressure from the attorneys general of New York, California, and Texas.

PR Doublespeak: First National Bank of Chicago reported $23 million as "nonperforming assets" in the bank's fourth-quarter financial statement for 1985.
Plain English: The bank was stuck with $23 million in overdrafts by a currency exchange and gold dealer in Jordan.

PR Doublespeak: Rolls-Royce officials say that on rare occasions one of their cars may "fail to proceed."
Plain English: Rolls Royces sometimes break down.

PR Doublespeak: Texas Instruments bragged that Massachusetts Institute of Technology had agreed to "acquire up to 400" new TI computers "under favorable terms" in 1984.
Plain English: TI donated 200 of the computers and discounted the rest.

PR Doublespeak: Trans Florida Airlines provided passengers on its Conair 240 airplanes with a card giving instructions "in case of a nonroutine operation."

Plain English: The airline handed out emergency instructions for use if the plane was about to crash.

PR Doublespeak: Wegmans Food Markets of Rochester, New York, advertised in 1985 for "part-time career associate scanning professionals."

Plain English: The company was hiring checkout clerks.

PR Doublespeak Question: What event were PR scribes describing when they talked of a "safety related occurrence" involving "rapid oxidation" and "energetic disassembly"?

Answer: General Public Utilities' near-disaster ("safety related occurrence") at Three Mile Island when fire ("rapid oxidation") and an explosion ("energetic disassembly") damaged the reactor core.

In Other Words, You're Fired

"Layoff" is such a nasty word that often companies order their PR departments to come up with another way of saying the same thing—such as nonretained, dehired, selected out, elimination of redundancies in the human resources area, and rationalization of marketing efforts. For the record, here are how some Misfortune 500 companies shamefully sidestepped the word "layoff":

AT&T couldn't bring itself to state plainly that employees in certain divisions were about to be laid off in 1986. The company announced that because of "surpluses" in various divisions, a new "force management plan" would be implemented to correct "force imbalances." Once "surplus managers" were identified, AT&T said, they "would be given a separation payment to leave." The company admitted that many of these separations would be of the "involuntary" kind.

Sun Oil Co., one of the nation's ten largest oil companies, claimed in 1985 that it did not lay off 40 of the 550 people employed at its headquarters. "We're managing our staff resources," said a spokesman. "Sometimes you manage them up, and sometimes you manage them down."

LTV Corp. denied it was laying off 600 workers at its Aliquippa, Pennsylvania, plant in 1985. Instead, LTV called the layoffs an "indefinite idling"—a euphemism which meant that LTV could avoid paying severance or pension benefits.

Faced with major layoffs in 1985, Control Data Corp. didn't want to announce the bad news. Instead, the firm told employees and the press that it was involved in ongoing assessments of the "skill mix" that would lead to company-wide "work-force adjustments."

To cut costs, Peak, Marwick, Mitchell & Co.—one of the nation's largest accounting firms—didn't want to initiate mass firings in 1985. So it announced that it would seek "requested departures" from twenty-six people.

International Telephone & Telegraph referred to its 1979 layoffs as "headcount reductions."

When mechanics went on strike against Continental Airlines in 1983, Continental said that the "strikers haven't been fired." However, the airlines added that it had begun hiring "permanent replacements."

The Franklin Mint did not lay off eighty workers in 1985, insisted a corporate spokesman. "We've had some realignments of positions and streamlining of operations," he explained.

Corporate Consultants Inc., a Tulsa firm that teaches companies how to fire people, says it provides "termination and outplacement consulting" for companies involved in "downsizing" and "reduction activities."

"YOU UNDERSTAND, OF COURSE, THIS IS NOT 'GOODBYE'... IT'S JUST THAT WE WON'T BE SAYING 'HELLO' TO EACH OTHER ANYMORE."

The PR Ploy That Backfired

General Motors tried a public relations gimmick that backfired in 1982.

Shortly after negotiations between the automaker and the United Auto Workers began, GM chairman Roger Smith and union chief Douglas Fraser held a press conference to announce that any savings generated by a wage-concession agreement would be passed on to consumers through reduced sticker prices.

So what happened? Thousands of customers postponed new GM car purchases until the labor agreement had been signed three months later.

Not the Real Thing

To promote the new soundtrack album of "Miami Vice" in 1985, MCA Records Canada sent reviewers copies of the record along with a little bag of white powder.

MCA thought it was a clever way to get everyone's attention. That it did—but not the kind the company wanted.

The powder was only sugar—not cocaine. However, it still left a bad taste in the mouths of critics who slammed MCA in the press for promoting the use of drugs. Even Toronto's deputy police chief, William McCormick, got in the act when he declared, "It's in poor taste—and that's not a pun about the sugar."

When the PR stunt backfired, Ross Reynolds, MCA Records Canada's executive vice-president, first told reporters that the bag of powder came from the company's U.S. parent, MCA Inc., in California. But upon further investigation, he discovered the idea was conceived in his own backyard. "Normally our promotions staff wouldn't have been that creative," he said. One MCA employee hinted that perhaps some reviewers were angered because the powder was not the real thing.

Reynolds insisted that the bag of powder wasn't meant to promote or condone drug use. He said the whole episode taught him not to make assumptions about people's sense of humor. "I've received a toy gun as a promotional gimmick," he said. "It certainly wasn't promoting murder."

Driving Off in a Huff

Like other auto companies, Buick lends cars to reviewers. But unlike the others, it took away the keys from one reviewing magazine which published a scathing critique of one of its models.

The automaker had proudly loaned *Car and Driver* magazine a 1987 Buick Riviera T Type for review. Buick expected to read words of praise. It didn't find any. The magazine said that while Buick was aiming for "a theme of understated elegance," it instead achieved "understated incoherence." A companion review said the car drove as smoothly as squeaking chalk.

This was not the kind of write-up that Buick wanted the public to read. To avoid getting panned further, the company simply took the car away from *Car and Driver* even though the magazine was only partway through its 30,000-mile test. The magazine claimed Buick's response was "thin-skinned" and industry sources said they couldn't recall any major auto company yanking one of its loaners from a reviewer.

Thomas L. Pond, Buick's director of public relations, took back the loaner because, he said, the magazine seemed to have had "a great dislike for the product and there wasn't any sense to spend another six months forcing them to put miles on it."

Perish(able) the Thought

Problem: How could the public relations firm of Ketchum MacLeod & Grove convince *The Wall Street Journal* to write a story about Arnold Bakers Inc.'s new preservative-free 100 percent wheat bread?

Solution: Mail the *Journal* three loaves of the bread.

Bigger Problem: When the bread was shipped from a packing house in Manhattan in June 1981, it took six days to reach the *Journal*'s newsroom in another part of Manhattan—just enough time for the bread to arrive covered with mold.

Ask and You Shall Deceive

To attract the press at a 1984 home builders' convention in Houston, Owens-Corning Fiberglass Corp. commissioned a survey on the industry's outlook.

The results were surprising and refuted most industry experts who expected construction to remain level throughout the year: the Owens-Corning survey showed that builders were planning a 30 percent increase in housing starts.

Armed with this happy news, the Owens-Corning PR staff called an elaborate news conference, complete with a panel of experts to analyze the survey results. But apparently none of the PR people bothered to ask the experts beforehand what they thought of the survey. They knew the poll was flawed because it was taken only among builders at the convention, who tended to be the largest and most aggressive companies.

Although the PR staff didn't question the panel, the reporters did, turning most of their attention to the star expert, Michael Sumichrast, chief economist for the National Association of Home Builders. When asked to interpret the Owens-Corning forecast, Sumichrast quickly dismissed it by saying: "Well, it shows when you ask stupid questions, you get stupid answers."

Raising a Stink

When the Elgin National Watch Co. was celebrating its centennial in 1961, it wanted to dramatize the company's involvement in space-age timing devices.

So the PR department came up with a gimmick that stunk to high heaven.

At the annual Retail Jewelers of America trade show in Manhattan, the company set up a tent and called it the "Moon Room." Models of NASA rockets and space craft were displayed along with examples of Elgin's space technology.

The PR people should have stopped there. Instead, they came up with a spaced-out plan. Since legend says the moon is made of green cheese, the PR staff bought a huge three-foot-wide wheel of Swiss cheese and placed it on a black velvet-covered table in the middle of the Moon Room.

But they hadn't considered a couple of factors—it was summer and the Moon Room was cooled by a single fan. After gratifying crowds for the grand-opening day, the wheel began to turn. The next day, the Elgin bigwigs arrived to check out the company's eye-catching exhibit. Instead, they were mortified to see showgoers fleeing from the Moon Room holding their noses.

Every Dog Has His Day

In the mid-1960s, the Chicago-based public relations firm of Harshe & Rotman Inc. barked up the wrong tree when it tried to promote Rival dog food's new all-beef dinner.

The agency decided to invite the press to a luncheon where the president of Rival and a pedigreed dog would share a table. "I felt uneasy about it because I knew that animals can be very unpredictable," recalled Morris Rotman, then chairman of the PR firm and now president of Ruder, Finn & Rotman Inc. "I was assured that the dog, a collie, was well trained and would be hungry."

Sure enough, with a mess of press on hand to witness the man-and-his-dog luncheon, the collie did what Rotman feared most—he turned his nose up on the new Rival food. No amount of coaxing could get the canine even to sniff it.

Finally, in desperation, the Rival president reached into the dog's bowl and ate the stuff himself—to the cheers of reporters.

The next day, the newspapers carried stories with headlines such as RIVAL PRESIDENT EATS DOG FOOD, BUT DOG WON'T. Rotman's embarrassed client took one look at the publicity and fired the agency. "I've never used an animal since," said Rotman.

Revenge of the Roaches

The Setup: Promote American Home Products' improved Black Flag insecticide containing Baygon by setting up a press conference. Spray one Petri dish full of cockroaches with Black Flag and another roach-infested dish with the competitor's Brand X. Watch the bugs sprayed with Black Flag drop dead faster.

The Payoff: The PR flacks are bugged beyond belief. The roaches don't die. Normally, insecticide is absorbed through the feet of skittering roaches. But those at the news conference are rendered lethargic by being in a chilly room and, thus, don't skitter; they just lie there.

The Post-mortem: "After thirty minutes of spraying the hell out of the damn things, the bugs were in better shape than I was," a PR man confided to *Dun's Review*. "All we could do was steer the press to the booze."

Check Out This Grocer's Line

What was the slick PR line used by Ralphs Grocery Co. when consumer resistance forced the Minneapolis chain to reverse its policy of making customers bag their own groceries?

Ralphs executive vice-president Al Marasca told the local press, "It was our intention to give customers the opportunity to participate in the shopping experience by bagging their own orders, which allowed us to maintain a lower price position. But because we try to run customer-driven stores, we've begun bagging all our orders."

Not Now

Morgan Guaranty Trust Co.'s public relations department issued this statement in November 1984, summarizing a speech by Denis Weatherstone, chairman of the bank's executive committee:

"Mr. Weatherstone emphasized that steps to reduce the federal deficit were not essential."

This correction came from the same public relations department the following day:

" 'Budget cutting steps are *now* essential,' said Mr. Weatherstone."

From an official of the public relations department:
"I'm sure Mr. Weatherstone was not amused."

Waste Not, Want Not

Sometimes a press release itself—rather than its words—can tell you a lot about a company. Several years ago, recipients of an announcement from Anadite Inc. learned that the Chicago firm wouldn't let anything go to waste.

In December 1979, the company mailed out a release saying that Felix T. Grossman had been elected chairman. The news was reported in business publications across the nation.

More than a year later, Anadite mailed out the same press release again. There was a good reason, said a spokesman. It seems that several unused copies of the announcement were found while cleaning out the corporate files, so Anadite sent them out again rather than pitch them. "We just wanted to remind people of the appointment," said the spokesman.

The Price Isn't Right

Osborne Computer Corp., which had been operating under the supervision of a federal bankruptcy court for a year, decided to do something new and different with its press kit in 1984—make reporters pay for it.

An invitation to an upcoming press conference told reporters that "there will be a modest charge" for receiving company news materials. An enclosed price list showed charges of $1.19 for a news release and $1.69 for a black-and-white photo of Osborne's new computer. "These nominal prices do entitle one to unlimited follow-up questions," the invitation continued.

Osborne really didn't expect the press to buy public relations. It was just a feeble attempt at humor—one that backfired badly. Thomas Mahon, the company's public relations director, explained: "We meant the invitation to show that despite its troubles, the company hadn't lost its sense of humor."

To the company's chagrin, it discovered that the press didn't share Osborne's sense of fun. Outraged reporters and editors called to complain about the unprecedented charges. One editor told Mahon, "If you can't afford to give a press conference, you're not worth writing about."

Cutting Losses

A company brochure is designed to promote the firm and provide as much information as possible.

But potential clients of T.A. Associates, a Boston venture capital company, wondered what the firm was trying to hide in 1984 when it mailed out brochures in which parts of pages 9 and 10 had been *cut out*.

The editing was a result of the departure of two partners. T.A. had printed up attractive brochures containing the photos and biographies of partners E. Roe Stamps IV and Stephen Woodsum. But when the pair resigned to start their own partnership, T.A. found itself stuck with the stack of brochures. Not wanting them to go to waste, management continued to mail out the brochures—but only after the photos and bios of the two departed company execs were excised from each one.

T.A. would have been better off just throwing away the brochures. Before getting new ones made up, the firm continued to send out the cut-up brochures, which listed an old address and put the company's total funds at an outdated $200 million—when it should have read $500 million.

Taking the Low Road

ROUTE 1

In 1984, Jartran Inc., the truck-renting firm, tried to ride roughshod over archrival U-Haul International.

As a "public service," Jartran's PR firm, Daniel J. Edelman Inc., sent a package of U-Haul internal memos and newspaper stories critical of their rival to several wire services and newspapers. A letter accompanying the package quoted a recent story on ABC-TV's "20/20" about wheels falling off U-Haul trucks. The letter also offered to supply more information about "this fascinating story."

There were no takers. When questioned about the PR ethics involved, Jartran's marketing director, Julio Siberio, said his company was just trying to alert the public to U-Haul's "dangerous" equipment.

ROUTE 2

Dow Chemical Co. played even dirtier. After members of Greenpeace, the worldwide environmentalist organization, plugged up effluent pipes at one of Dow's Michigan plants in 1985, the company had some of the protesters arrested. That was within Dow's rights. But what its PR staff did next was way out of line.

Through illegally leaked information, Dow learned that a blood test of one of the Greenpeace members indicated the possible presence of venereal disease. An overzealous Dow public relations executive then called a local activist to tell her the news. She took this as a crass intimidation tactic to silence the activists.

She went public with the conversation—and Dow PR flacks went stammering for the right words to halt a flurry of unwanted newspaper coverage. Spokesmen finally agreed on a stance—the company only wanted to locate the individual so she could get treatment. (She subsequently was found free of the disease.)

The Detroit Free Press said it best by writing that Dow's actions stemmed from "base orneriness."

DEMOTIONS FOR PROMOTIONS

MARKETING HYPE THAT BACKFIRED

The Saga of Pan Am's "Bottle in the Basket" Promotion

CHAPTER 1
To demonstrate Pan Am's superior service on the hotly competitive New York–San Juan route, the airline's ad agency, J. Walter Thompson, comes up with a cute idea: The airline will serve passengers a small bottle of Mateus wine, sliced salami, cheese, and an apple in a little plastic basket on a dainty gingham tablecloth. Newspaper ads are prepared to announce the promotion.

CHAPTER 2
All of a sudden, the agency receives a hysterical phone call from Pan Am: "Don't run the ads! We just received 2,000 pounds of sliced salami—but our contract with the commissary requires that all meats must be sliced by them." The ads are canceled. Meanwhile, back goes the sliced salami and out goes a rush order for a ton of whole salamis.

CHAPTER 3
The whole salamis arrive and are sliced in the commissary. The ads are set to run. Suddenly, another crisis erupts. Pan Am issues a May Day call—the bottles of wine are in San Juan but the little plastic baskets are in New York. The ads are postponed until the bottles catch up with the baskets.

CHAPTER 4
There's a mix-up in the order. The baskets are shipped to San Juan at the same time the wine is being flown to New York.

CHAPTER 5
Finally, the logistics problems are straightened out and Pan Am orders JWT to run the kickoff ads. The flight is a sellout and the airline and ad agency rejoice. But their happiness is short-lived. Word comes that the wine bottles aboard the maiden flight have cork tops, not screw-off caps, and the flight attendants have no corkscrews to open them. More than 180 passengers are ready to break the bottles over the flight attendants' heads.

CHAPTER 6
Pan Am ships cases of Mateus back to Portugal in exchange for screw-capped bottles. Finally, all the elements in the promotion are in place—except one. Pan Am switches its Puerto Rico service to much larger 747s, and the assembly and service of baskets of food for 300 passengers is deemed too much of a hassle for the flight attendants. Pan Am ditches the promotion.

Bank Promotions That Deserved to Draw Fire

South Umpqua State Bank, with branches in southwestern Oregon, offered a .240 caliber Weatherby Magnum Mark V Rifle—a "high velocity masterpiece"—for anyone (except, presumably, bank robbers) depositing more than $1,000 in a savings account in 1980.

North Carolina National Bank, of Winston-Salem, offered a special credit arrangement in 1981 to help fund the National Rifle Association. Each NRA member who signed up could open special accounts at a discount and have personalized checks printed with a picture of a shotgun. In addition, the bank would pay the NRA .05 percent of the cash value of purchases made by members with the bank's credit card. Considering that this promotion came shortly after assassination attempts on President Reagan and Pope John Paul II, the plan was shot down within two months.

Bohemian Savings and Loan, of St. Louis, offered a veritable armament to customers in 1983. Hoping to attract long-term deposits by paying interest with guns instead of dollars, Bohemian offered new depositors several Browning and Weatherby shotguns, rifles, and accessories.

Bank of Findley, in Findley, Illinois, was lucky none of its customers asked a teller, "Give me a gun—and your money too." To increase business in 1983, the bank offered new depositors of $2,500 or more handguns as a premium. Customers had their choice of a Colt Python .357 or a Colt Diamond .22.

"I'M SURE IT IS, AS YOU SAY, 'A SWEET LITTLE BABY,' MR. PERKINS... BUT I WAS REALLY HOPING FOR A TOASTER."

What was the flaw in United Airlines' "Fly Your Wife Free" campaign in which businessmen were encouraged to bring their wives along gratis?

When businessmen took advantage of the promotion, United sent letters of appreciation to their spouses. Soon the airline was inundated with angry letters from outraged wives who said they had never been off the ground and demanded to know the names of their high-flying husbands' companions.

They Said It Would Never Fly...

Pacific Air Lines, a small, but enterprising, West Coast commuter carrier, wanted an attention-grabbing campaign that would send profits soaring. Instead, PAL ran commercial aviation's most ill-conceived promotion—one that sent the company into a tailspin.

In 1967, PAL sought the help of irreverent comedian Stan Freberg, who moonlighted as a Los Angeles–based ad consultant. Freberg suggested that PAL poke fun at the one thing all other airlines never mention—fear of flying. Many of the carrier's executives were aghast and warned that the campaign would go down in flames. But PAL's president, Matthew McCarthy, told Freberg to fly with the idea.

Under the comedian's direction, PAL placed full-page ads in New York and Los Angeles newspapers that read, "Hey there! You with the sweat in your palms. It's about time an airline faced up to something: most people are scared witless of flying. Deep down inside, every time that big plane lifts off that runway, you wonder if this is it, right? You want to know something, fella? So does the pilot deep down inside."

But PAL, at Freberg's urging, didn't stop there. It added some zany touches on its flights to help people laugh at their fears. Flight attendants gave passengers survival kits that contained a pink rabbit's foot, Norman Vincent Peale's *The Power of Positive Thinking,* and an unappetizing fortune cookie that held the message, "It could be worse. The pilot could be whistling 'The High and the Mighty.'" Also, whenever the plane touched down, flight attendants were told to say in loud voices, "We made it! How about that?"

To give shaky airborne passengers a feeling that they were still on the ground, PAL planned to draw the cabin shades and project pictures of telephone poles going by. PAL also had plans to paint the outside of one of its 727s to look like an old steam locomotive complete with wheels and cow catcher. The sounds of a locomotive would play throughout the passenger cabin. "On the outside, people are Bogart all the way," said Freberg. "But inside, they are Peter Lorre trapped in a Casablanca hotel room with no hope of escape and sweating profusely."

Not surprisingly, the airline industry was in an uproar. Executives from other carriers feared the promotion was scaring potential customers away from all airlines. But PAL's McCarthy scoffed at the critics, saying, "Lots of people are terrified of flying and we thought it was time somebody cleared the air."

The bizarre promotion did clear the air—of PAL planes. Within two months, the airline was no more.

Recipe for One Nerd on Wry—To Go

INGREDIENTS:

creative juices from J. Walter Thompson ad agency
40 million dollars from Burger King
1 Herb

Mix the creative juices of the ad agency with all those Burger King dollars until you have created an advertising campaign that will feature the only person in America who has never tasted a Whopper—Herb. Now add Herb and dress him in glasses, gaudy plaids, and white socks with untied shoes. Stir public interest by cooking up a contest in which consumers win $5,000 if they spot Herb hanging out at the local Burger King. Half-bake this idea for several months until you notice that sales increase by only 1 percent. Then throw the whole campaign out. No one will swallow it anyway.

Offsides

Beatrice Companies Inc. ran a contest during the 1985 football season called "Monday Night Winning Lineup."

Scratch cards for the game were available in display cases in grocery stores. On the cards were two rows of dots. Contestants had to randomly scratch the right spot to find the correct number of touchdowns and field goals for eight Monday night games. (The game could be played after the scores were in.) Contestants could also win cash and merchandise. The grand prize: a trip, valued at $20,000, for eight people by Learjet to the Super Bowl.

In the course of entering hundreds of cards, Frank Maggio, an Atlanta salesman who had taken a college course in game theory, began to notice that particular numbers kept appearing in the same spots on different cards. When he figured out the possible patterns, Maggio and his partner Jim Curl began hauling home grocery bags full of contest cards. They scratched thousands of cards and, by the contest deadline, they had mailed in 4,000 winning entries.

With "winnings" reaching the cash equivalent of more than $20 million, Maggio and Curl approached Beatrice and offered to settle for $1 million in cash. Beatrice turned them down flat. Then the giant corporation ran newspaper ads announcing the whole contest was canceled because the game had been compromised since entry blanks might have been obtained "unfairly."

Maggio and Curl filed suit under the Fair Trade Practices Act seeking $21.3 million in actual damages—the amount they say they won in cash and prizes. The suit was settled out of court. Terms of the agreement remained confidential.

Why did wise travelers question the credibility of Braniff's 1984 promotion that passengers' next round-trip flight on the airline could earn them two free tickets to Hawaii?

Braniff didn't fly to Hawaii, nor did the three other carriers listed as participants in the promotion.

In the Red Sauce

Officials at Ragu Foods Inc. turned redder than their spaghetti sauce when they ran a contest in 1986 that turned into a recipe for disaster.

In newspaper ads across the country, Ragu touted a simple game involving three labels of Ragu products. "Match the symbols below on this official game card to a Ragu Spaghetti Sauce package at your favorite grocer," said the ad. The prizes ranged from $100 to $1,000, depending on the number of symbols that matched exactly.

Ragu, which expected to give away $200,000 in total prize money, said that the odds of winning $1,000 were 1-in-385,000. However, much to their shock, officials discovered a printing error right after the contest began. The misprint reduced the odds to 1-in-1!

Shuddering at the thought of paying millions of dollars because every card would have been a winner, Ragu canceled the whole promotion.

Enter This Contest at Your Own Risk

There were several important questions to ponder in a 1981 promotional contest run by Northwest Airlines. The grand, and only, prize was the use of an entire Boeing 727 jet for a trip to Fort Lauderdale, Florida, airline transportation home, and three nights in a luxury hotel for ninety-three people.

The airline trumpeted the contest in full-page ads in Midwest newspapers that said, "Win a jet to Florida and take 92 friends along ... Take your relatives. Take your co-workers. Take your church group, lodge or neighbors."

Now for the questions:

Q. Who didn't Northwest suggest taking along, but should have?
A. The winner's accountant.

Q. Why should the winner take his accountant?
A. So the accountant could explain what Northwest failed to mention—the winner could lose his shirt.

Q. How could the winner end up a loser?
A. The prizes in all such contests constitute taxable income. The winner of the Northwest promotion would be forced to cover the added taxable income for his friends. If the winner made use of the full value of the prize, he would add $50,000 to his taxable income for 1981.

Q. How did Northwest try to compensate for this?
A. On the advice of its tax attorneys, the airline threw in $15,000 to help the winner pay this added tax burden.

Q. Was there anything wrong with that?
A. The cash gift itself was also taxable.

Q. What finally happened?
A. The winner skipped the free jet trip and took a cash settlement.

What company had an ulterior motive when it offered consumers a free booklet of hot and spicy recipes?
Miles Laboratories, maker of Alka-Seltzer.

The Fine Print

Some winners of Corning Glass Works' 1985 sweepstakes were not so happy.

True, they had won fourth prize, which was a bottle of perfume, but they were still ticked off by the contest rules. The rules stated "No Purchase Necessary" in bold-face type. No problem there. But then, in fine print, it said, "See Rule 2 to claim prize." And what did Rule 2 say? "To claim prize, mail . . . $2.00 plus 2 proofs of purchase . . ."

BADVERTISING CAMPAIGNS

ADS THAT NEVER SHOULD HAVE RUN

From Hero to Zero

No commercial was ever more offensive to women or fatal to the product it was hawking than the TV spot for a detergent called Hero.

In 1969, Lever Brothers introduced Hero—and then quickly killed it because its sexist TV commercial went overboard in glorifying housewives' unbridled adoration of a mere box of soap.

The TV spot, produced by the Doyle Dane Bernbach ad agency, depicted a twenty-five-foot-tall soap box bearing the imposing likeness of a stone-carved Greek god with a booming macho male voice. Clustered around the base of the box was a horde of writhing, glassy-eyed, moaning women whose arms were raised and waving in supplication to "their hero." The women gazed in awe as the voice-over said, "I, Hero, am here. I am the strong detergent with the yet-unheard-of power ... I clean with strength ... Your hands will feel the soft. Friends, housewives, countrywomen, bring me your wash."

By this time, the women could barely contain themselves. They began jumping around and shouting, "I wanna Hero kind of clean. I wanna strong yet softer clean. I wanna see it. I wanna feel it. Want my eyes to see the clean. Want my hands to feel the soft."

It was enough to choke even a male chauvinist.

BADVERTISING QUIZ

(Match the advertising gimmick with the product)

1. body in coffin	A. batteries
2. minister	B. National Rifle Association
3. naked baby	C. corporate condominiums
4. priest and monk	D. wood paneling
5. train bearing down on car straddling tracks	E. brandy

(TURN PAGE FOR ANSWERS)

Answers:

1–C: In 1985, the Cuyahoga Group chose to promote its new Florida corporate retreat, Pierre-Par-La-Mer, by running an ad in business magazines that featured an executive laid out in a coffin under a headline that called the scene THE ULTIMATE IN CORPORATE STRESS. It was a grave mistake. It caused such a negative response that the ad was pulled.

2–B: A 1985 National Rifle Association ad pictured the Reverend Dr. Stacy Groscup, in cleric's collar, holding a rifle and saying, "I'm the NRA." Shouldn't a minister be preaching the word of God instead of plugging a gun lobby?

3–D: Somehow, States Industries Inc. found a way of linking a naked baby to a pitch for wood paneling in a 1983 ad. Under the headline DON'T THROW OUT THE BABY WITH THE BATH WATER, there was a picture of an infant flying through an open window with the wash. The only thing that should have been tossed out was the idea for this atrocious ad.

4–E: Glenmore Distilleries, distributor of liquors throughout the northeast, presented a shameless ad in 1986 that exploited the use of wine in Catholic ceremony. The ad, in Spanish, featured a priest and a monk gazing heavenward with glasses of Felipe II brandy in hand. The copy, when translated, read, "To drink it is not a sin."

5–A: It was easy to understand why the TV networks at first refused to broadcast GNB Industries' 1985 commercial touting Champion batteries. In the TV spot, a spokesman stood next to his car which was straddling railroad tracks. He calmly extolled the fast-start virtues of Champion batteries as a train sped toward him. At the last moment, he jumped in, started the car, and sped to safety. The networks ran the commercial only after a disclaimer was added warning people not to try the stunt. Even so, consumer and safety groups caused such an uproar that the commercial was yanked.

What company apparently spent too much time in the boys' locker room when it ran an ad in 1983 headlined, IT TAKES MORE THAN BIG CHESTS AND NICE JUGS TO ATTRACT CUSTOMERS?

The King-Seeley Thermos Co., whose outrageously offensive headline accompanied a photo of various Thermos containers.

> Why did Frank Sellinger, CEO of Joseph Schlitz Brewing Co., stop appearing in TV ads in 1981 after he asked viewers to compare his beer with his competitors' brews?
>
> Sellinger was receiving too many calls in the middle of the night from overly enthusiastic Schlitz drinkers reporting their own taste tests.

Most A-Peeling Sales Pitch of 1986

In 1986, Silo, a discount appliance-store chain, ran a TV commercial for a stereo it claimed cost only "299 bananas." Sure enough, dozens of customers in Seattle and El Paso took the TV spots literally and brought in 11,000 bananas.

Silo honored the fruity currency, lost $10,465 on the stereos—and slipped its TV spots off the air.

> Who was paid by Gillette for five years *not* to appear in its commercials?
>
> Record-setting 1972 Olympic gold medal swimmer Mark Spitz. After signing a lucrative deal with Gillette, Mark sank as a TV pitchman, so he took the money and swam off.

Iacocca's Edsel

In nationally run print ads in 1985, Lee Iacocca urged Americans to write Washington to oppose the lowering of fuel efficiency standards for automakers.

The Chrysler chairman wanted everyone to believe that he was spearheading a grass-roots movement to conserve energy. But his campaign backfired when too many people realized it was a ploy to enlist the government against his competitors.

It all began when the National Highway Traffic Safety Administration wanted a change in the law that would allow automakers to lower the average gas mileage of their new cars from 27.5 miles per gallon to 26 miles per gallon. That delighted General Motors and Ford, which manufacture most of the big cars in America and couldn't meet the new standard. But Iacocca wanted the law strictly enforced for a self-serving reason—Chrysler sells a greater proportion of smaller cars than its two major rivals.

To bolster sales of his new small cars, Iacocca ordered $225,000 worth of newspaper and magazine ads disguised as public service messages. He wanted to whip up public support for the law. But the response wasn't exactly what Iacocca had in mind. Half the letters sent to the highway traffic administration were from riled big-car lovers who vehemently disagreed with Iacocca. The "public service" ad campaign generated only 500 letters backing him. That meant Chrysler spent a whopping $450 for each letter of support.

> What company had the audacity to use a song about avoiding paternity suits for its TV commercial jingle?
> Pepsi. It transformed Michael Jackson's hit "Billie Jean" into the sound of the new Pepsi Generation in 1984.

The Timing Was Just a Little Bit Off

United American Bank of Louisville launched a major campaign in 1983 with the theme "United We Stand."

Three Days Later: The bank collapsed.

Eastern Airlines boasted in a 1981 ad that its "people have something 18,000 other airline people don't. A job. Because last year, while other airlines laid off almost 18,000 people, Eastern actually added some . . . At Eastern, we believe that you shouldn't have to give up service just because times are tough."

Two Days Earlier: The wire services reported, "Eastern Airlines Inc. will trim its work force by 3,000 employees, half through layoffs . . ."

Continental Airlines ran print ads in 1983 saying, "Celebrate the Birth of Our New Airline."

One Day Earlier: It must have been a painful labor—Continental went into Chapter 11 proceedings and slashed its staff, cutting the pay of those who remained.

Eastern Airlines ran a radio commercial in 1985 offering cut-rate fares on a "new reorganized Eastern Airlines."

One Day Later: Eastern sheepishly admitted that it had accidentally promoted itself as a company already in bankruptcy court proceedings. When it had fallen into technical default on its $2.1 billion long-term debt because talks with its labor unions had faltered, the airline commissioned the radio commercial. However, Eastern worked out a new labor agreement that staved off bankruptcy—but the airline forgot to pull the commercial.

It Was Just a Little Oversight

To celebrate the economic recovery of the Midwest in 1984, AmeriTrust Corp., the Cleveland-based bank holding firm, placed ads citing three companies whose new technology was forging "the renaissance of industry in MidAmerica."

The ads were a nice idea, but they lacked the necessary veracity.

The ads boasted that one of the companies, the Hunt Steel Co., subsidiary of Hunt Energy Co., had "set up a modern mini-mill in an abandoned plant in Youngstown [Ohio] and is competing successfully by using the latest computer-controlled . . . technology."

Unfortunately, that just wasn't true. What was true was that AmeriTrust and its ad agency had not checked out the facts. Hunt Steel had shut down eight months earlier because it couldn't pay a $564,000 gas bill. Then, four months later, its parent, Hunt Energy, filed for Chapter 11 bankruptcy law protection.

The ad was prepared by Edward Howard & Co., a Cleveland agency whose chairman John T. Bailey admitted, "It was an oversight."

How did Pfeiffers Brewing Co. discover that advertising copy for print doesn't always work for radio?

When it ran—and then quickly pulled—its commercial that trumpeted Pfeiffers as "the beer with the silent P."

An Appel for the Teacher

An Apple Computer ad was short-circuited by an embarrassing glitch caused by its ad agency, BBDO/New York.

The agency created an ad that hailed the Apple II as "the leading computer in education" and then misspelled a word. The ad, which ran in major publications in 1986, showed a classroom with a blackboard note reminding students of a quiz "tommorrow."

What did Apple do after seeing the gaffe?

It sent BBDO's art director his own Apple II—with a built-in spellchecker.

Guilt by Association

EXHIBIT 1
Piedmont Airlines wanted to promote an association between itself and college football, so it ran an ad in 1981 in football programs at more than forty colleges. The ad featured a photo of Notre Dame football coach Knute Rockne—a rather bizarre choice considering that he was killed with seven others in a plane crash in 1931. When the blunder was called to the attention of W. G. McGee, Piedmont's senior vice-president, he said Rockne had been included "because of his personality, not how he left this world."

EXHIBIT 2
In print ads, Anheuser-Busch depicted its Baybry's champagne cooler as having been served at a party celebrating the flight of the "Spruce Goose," Howard Hughes's monstrous airplane. But the ad gave the subliminal message that the cooler was associated with a lemon—one of the biggest flops in aviation history. The eight-engine, all-wood flying boat flew only once in 1947—for a distance of less than a mile at a height of only seventy feet.

It Lost Something in the Translation

When companies try to sell their products in foreign countries, sometimes their advertising—when translated too literally—doesn't quite get the message across. Misfortune 500 companies have found that advertising in foreign lands can bring them more embarrassment than business. For example:

When General Motors Corp. ran ads in Belgium ballyhooing "Body by Fisher," the literal Flemish translation was "Corpse by Fisher."

Schweppes Tonic Water had to shorten its name in Italy to Schweppes Tonica because "il water" is idiomatic Italian for bathroom.

Pepsico once ran into translation troubles in Germany when consumers there interpreted Pepsi's "come alive" ad campaign to mean "arise from the grave."

Coca-Cola Co. had to change its name in China in 1986 after it discovered that its phonetic equivalent, *"Ke Kou Ke La,"* meant "Bite the wax tadpole."

General Motors Corp. couldn't understand why sales were so dismal in Latin America after the automaker introduced its new economy car, the Nova. Finally, GM wised up and realized that in Spanish, *"no va"* means "it doesn't go."

The Naked Truth about Braniff's Hispanic Ad Campaign

In an effort to encourage Hispanics in the United States to fly Braniff Airlines, an ad campaign in 1987 left people believing they would fly naked.

The ad, run on Spanish-language television and radio stations, touted Braniff's leather seats. The radio commercial told listeners to fly Braniff *"en cuero,"* which means "in leather." But a very similar Spanish expression, *"en cueros,"* means "naked"—and the two phrases sound identical when spoken quickly.

Even more eye-opening was the TV commercial version, which invited travelers to fly *"en cuero"* and *"con tres pulgadas mas,"* meaning "with three inches more." Presumably the airline was referring to the extra leg room, but those people who thought the voice-over said *"en cueros"* received an entirely different message.

UNTRUTH IN ADVERTISING

MISLEADING THE CONSUMER

They Should Have Their Asterisks Kicked*

*How Companies Use an Innocent Symbol and
Fine Print to Mislead Consumers*

Victor Technologies Inc. placed newspaper ads in 1986 that were headlined, "For $2495*, what you see is what you get." The picture showed a Victor V286 personal computer with monitor and video board.

*"Does not include monitor or video board."

Resort Investment Corp., of Columbia, South Carolina, ran a 1986 newspaper ad promising fully furnished, two-bedroom, two-bath resort condos on Atlantic City's Boardwalk for only $89,900 each.

fine print: It would cost you $89,900 if you could find two other friends, associates, or relatives to each fork over $89,900 because actual condo prices started at $269,700.

Ramada Renaissance Hotel in Denver tried to lure guests with a 1985 newspaper ad that promised in bold letters, "Free Hotel Room." But then the dreaded asterisk popped up in the copy.

*"Parking $55.00/night (Parking is mandatory)"

Magnussen-Barbee, a Ford-Lincoln-Mercury dealer in Napa, California, ran a newspaper ad in 1986 featuring five cars and a truck. Under each vehicle was a great price and the word "invoice" in large type—with an asterisk.

*"Invoice Amounts Given for Information Only. Does Not Reflect Selling Price."

Marvin Les-Lee, an electrical-appliance dealer in Great Neck, New York, listed a Caloric built-in oven with an attractive price of $289.88.

> fine print: Oven doors are extra.

Louisiana Savings, of Baton Rouge, ran an ad in 1986 headlined, "Free Checking Account."*

> *"$200 minimum balance required for free service charge. First 25 checks processed free, thereafter, 15 cents per check."

Harry Smith Woodworking, in Hellam, Pennsylvania, offered consumers a "free waterbed" in a 1986 newspaper ad.

> fine print: You had to buy a fill-and-drain kit worth $3 for $159.

Ma Bell's Shell Game

Hundreds of thousands of Bell system customers plunked down $65 to $175 in 1980 for Design Line phones that came in offbeat shapes like Mickey Mouse and an old-fashioned country crank model.

A year later, these buyers learned that they didn't really own those phones at all—they owned only a plastic shell. Bell retained title to the mechanical innards.

Customers received the rude awakening in June 1981 when Bell's operating subsidiaries told the phone shell owners they could buy the working mechanism for $30. The customers also discovered that they had been paying monthly service charges of as much as $2.15 for phones they thought they owned.

"I was outraged," one customer told *The Wall Street Journal*. "It's like buying a car and having Ford bill you later for the engine and transmission." Said another, "I'm not about to spend $65 for four ounces of plastic."

AT&T insisted that it "was very clear and up-front" in advising customers that Bell would retain title to the telephone's working parts. In fact, added the company, the following information was spelled out right on the phone: "The telephone housing is your property. To assure quality, all working parts . . . remain the property and responsibility of the Bell Telephone Co."

What the company failed to mention is that this information was printed on a 1-by-1½-inch label on the bottom of the phone in type 1/16th of an inch high.

Check This Out

Household Finance Corp. preyed on people who were short of cash during the 1985 holiday season.

The company launched a devious direct-mail campaign that unfairly exploited consumers' desire for fast money by sending them unsolicited $1,500 checks during the Christmas rush. These checks, which had to be cashed before December 25, became automatic, high-interest loans. A letter accompanying each check said it was "just our way of showing you how quick and convenient it is to get money from HFC!"

What the letter didn't say, but an enclosed fine-print Truth-in-Lending Disclosure did, was that the loan came with a whopping interest rate of nearly 22 percent—higher than common credit cards.

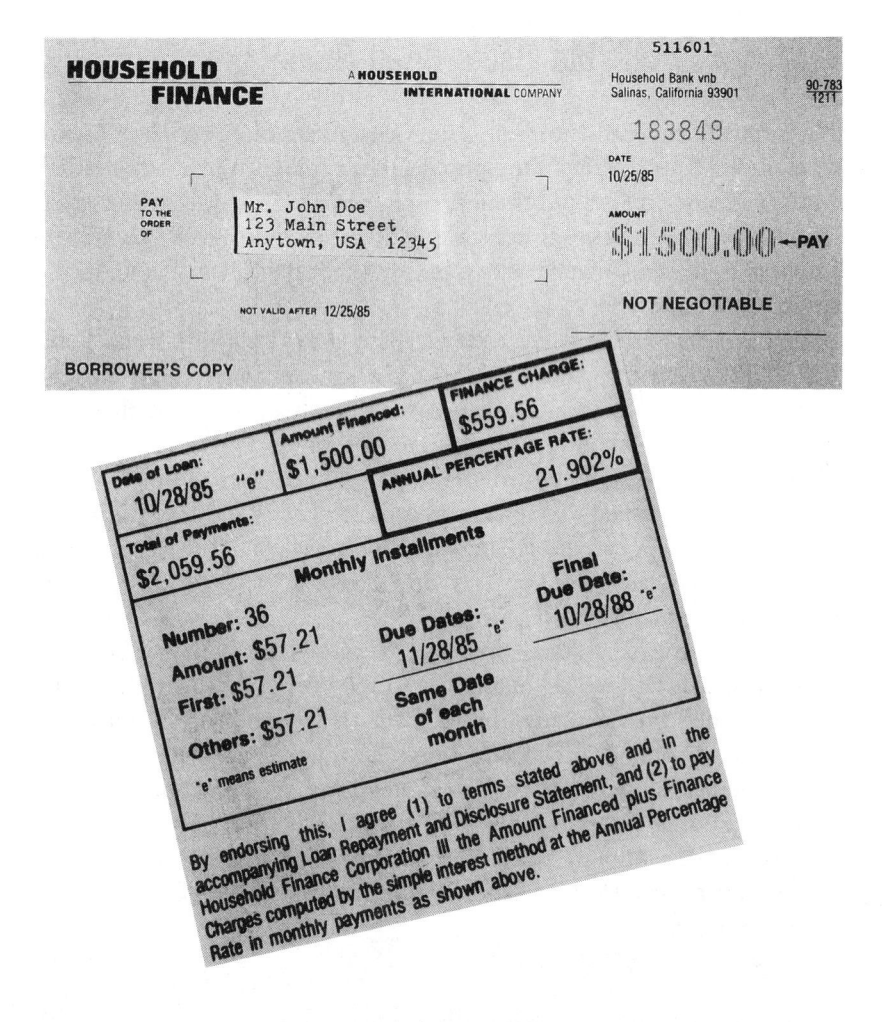

Stamp of Disapproval

*Other Examples of Irresponsible
Direct-Mail Advertising*

Wells Fargo Bank sent out mailings in 1986 offering to sell its California consumers protection against lost or stolen credit cards. For $12 a year, the bank stated, "Hotline Credit Card Protection reimburses you for up to $5,000 per incident." However, state law required sellers of credit-card insurance to notify prospective buyers that a person's liability for unauthorized use of a lost or stolen credit card is limited to only $50. So where was Wells Fargo's notice? On the inside surface of the envelope.

Shell Oil Co., in 1986, mailed its customers an envelope that said, "Important Reminder for Shell Credit Cardholder." It also said, "Pre-Cancellation Notice." Concerned recipients ripped open the envelope only to discover that inside was a soon-to-expire offer for a credit-card protection plan that Shell wanted to sell.

Regency Olds in Lakewood, New Jersey, sent out a postcard in 1985 with the return address of GM Protection Plan Headquarters, P.O. Box C, c/o Regency Olds, Lakewood, New Jersey. Its message was cause for concern: "URGENT! Please call at your earliest convenience ... [and] have your General Motors Manufacturers Warranty Book in hand." The card then listed a toll-free phone number. Was this an important safety recall? Nope. It was a sneaky Regency Olds sales pitch for an extended warranty.

Judging for Yourself

In its mail-order consumer catalogs, Hammacher Schlemmer & Co. has proclaimed that it sells nothing but the best. It has offered "the best waffle iron," "the best electric wok," and "the best home answering machine" among many other "bests."

And the company backs up its claims by "independent" testing. So what could be misleading? Hammacher Schlemmer's definition of "independent."

In a 1986 promotional letter to potential customers, the company's chairman, John R. MacArthur, said that a "completely separate" independent, nonprofit "consumer" organization tests and compares all the products. However, he failed to mention a few facts such as:

• The testing organization is called the Hammacher Schlemmer Institute.
• The institute is funded by Hammacher Schlemmer & Co.
• The institute's board of directors is composed of Hammacher Schlemmer officials.
• The institute is located at Hammacher Schlemmer company headquarters in Chicago.

Hammacher Schlemmer CEO Richard Tinberg told *The Wall Street Journal* the institute is a separate division that evaluates a product regardless of such internal influences as the company's profit margin or inventory level. That allows customers to make "intelligent and informed purchasing decisions," he said. But at its New York store, some signs placed next to various products were hardly informative. They told shoppers the items were declared the "best" by comparison testing—without mentioning who did the testing.

To paraphrase Snow White's evil stepmother, "Mirror, mirror, on the wall, who sells the best products of them all?" You do, Hammacher Schlemmer, because the Hammacher Schlemmer Institute says so.

Unreal People in Real Situations

John Hancock Mutual Life Insurance Co.'s "Real Life, Real Answers" TV commercials in 1986 and 1987 led viewers to believe that, as the company said, "real people in real situations" were giving details of their personal finances.

For example, there was John Wilder, a personnel director who made $43,000, and his homemaker wife Sandy. The commercial said the couple "came to us recently for our recommendations on ways to both supplement their income and accumulate capital to provide for their children's education." Then there was Linda Fuller, a divorced librarian who earned $20,000 and received $6,000 in child support. She was worried that she wouldn't have enough money to pay for her child's education when he grew up. "And somehow ... you know ... I've got to pull it off ... and I've got to do it myself," she said solemnly.

When asked how John Hancock found customers willing to reveal so much about their personal finances on national television, company spokesman Ralph Brunner admitted that the people featured in the commercials were actors. "In that sense," he said, "they are not real people."

Real People in an Unreal Situation

First American Bank of Virginia took out a full-page ad in several major newspapers in 1982 that showed a photograph of the bank's four top officers standing in the heart of Manhattan's financial district.

The ad's headline read: "We're looking the big boys right in the eye." The ad, which said that companies didn't "have to go to a city like New York" for their banking needs, included a caption of the bank officers that began: "Pictured on Wall Street ..."

The truth is that the officers were photographed in a Washington, D.C., studio. Their pictures were then trimmed and superimposed on a photo of Wall Street. Said Rick Barrow, creative director at Woods & Co., the bank's ad agency, "We're not trying to fool anybody. They're not literally there. That's why we made a point to say *pictured* on Wall Street."

Birth Pangs

To promote the 1986 Plymouth, Chrysler Corp. launched an advertising campaign designed to tug at the patriotic soul of the American consumer. The campaign was called "Born in America."

Commercials featured a Bruce Springsteen–like singer belting out a rousing jingoistic ballad as scenes of Plymouths shared airtime with cuts of flag raising, Niagara Falls, and amber waves of grain. Naturally, viewers were led to believe that Plymouths were built in the U.S.A.

But not all Plymouths were—or are—born here. The Voyager minivan, one of Plymouth's most popular vehicles, is made in Windsor, Ontario. Not only that, but most Voyagers come with a four-cylinder engine made in Japan by Mitsubishi. How does Chrysler explain this contradiction? A. C. Liebler, Plymouth's general marketing manager, told reporters, "It's a born-in-America campaign—and Canada is in North America." His boss, Joseph Campana, Chrysler's vice-president of marketing, insisted that the vehicles were born in the U.S.—because they were *designed* here.

However, in fairness to Chrysler, there was one time when the carmaker did make the distinction between the cars it builds here and in Canada. In some 1986 print ads, Chrysler offered rebates "on every car and truck we build in America." But the fine print in the ads said the minivan was excluded. "America in this sense means the United States," said a spokesman.

How Companies Fool Some of the People Some of the Time

HEWLETT-PACKARD
In print ads in 1984-85, Hewlett-Packard said its $120 HP12C calculator met "FDIC and Regulation Z standards for accuracy."

The Truth: Any calculator on the market will meet the FDIC and Regulation Z standards for accuracy.

KENNER PRODUCTS
In the toy company's 1985 commercials touting Upsy Baby, little children pulled the doll's string and pushed a button and gleefully watched Upsy Baby stand up all by herself.

The Truth: Kids needed Mommy or Daddy to make the doll operate because it required following a complicated eight-step instruction manual.

ARBY'S
In a $25 million ad campaign in 1985, Arby's urged consumers to "go for the lean" and be on "the lean team" by eating Arby's "lean advantage" roast beef sandwiches.

The Truth: Arby's roast beef *meat*—not its *sandwich*—was low in fat. The Bac'n Cheddar Deluxe, featured in the ad campaign, contained 561 calories, more than half from fat. That's the equivalent of eight teaspoons of fat.

UNIDEN CORPORATION OF AMERICA
Uniden depicted a label with the words "FCC Approved" in 1985 print ads for its cordless telephones.

The Truth: The Federal Communications Commission does not "approve" phones at all. Nor does it grade their quality. The FCC registers phones merely to establish minimum compatibility standards for phone manufacturers—not for consumers.

UNITED STATES MAP CO.
In 1981, the company promoted "a huge mural map of the United States of America that measures 828 square inches."

The Truth: A little math proves that the "huge" map was smaller than two feet by three feet.

PURITY SUPREME INC.

The large New England grocery chain launched a campaign in 1984 to promote locally grown tomatoes by giving away a free book of recipes, all calling for fresh tomatoes.

The Truth: The book was prepared by the *Florida* tomato exchange.

Sweetening the Deal

You would think that Sweet 'n Low soda is sweetened with nothing but Sweet 'n Low. But that's not so.

The soda is also sweetened with NutraSweet, a Sweet 'n Low *competitor*. MBC Beverage Inc., which licensed the Sweet 'n Low name from Cumberland Packing Corp., discovered that consumers wanted the natural sweetener NutraSweet rather than the artificial saccharin of Sweet 'n Low. So MBC sweetened Sweet 'n Low soda with NutraSweet. How did MBC get away with this? A spokesman said the company was well within its rights because "our contractual responsibility is to be a low-calorie soft drink."

Check the Label

General Mills emblazoned boxes of Kix corn puffs in 1987: "New better taste! Ask your kids!" and also "Low in sugar." On the back was a message addressed to Mom: "How can new Kix cereal taste so incredibly good and *still* be low in sugar? Here's the secret: . . . we did find a way to move the little bit of sugar from the inside of the Kix puff to the outside." But the real secret comes when you compare the fine print of the new and old nutrition labeling. General Mills increased the sugar content from two to three grams per ounce.

Lowes Co. put this comforting statement on the box of its Environtemp ceiling fan: "Designed for quick 'Do-It-Yourself' installation with ordinary tools (detailed instructions inside)." The instructions inside are so detailed that they recommend the fan be installed by a qualified electrician.

Turtle Wax Inc.'s Turtle Wax Power Brite, a cleaner for custom mag car wheels, clearly stated on its label in 1985: "New, safe . . . contains no acid." However, at the bottom of the label, it read: "Danger: flammable, corrosive, and toxic. Causes burns to eyes or skin on contact. Fatal or harmful if swallowed."

Sargento Cheese Co.'s Sargento 100 Percent Natural Grated Italian Style Cheeses isn't. Its primary ingredient, according to the label, is grated Swiss cheese.

Nybco made a wood-refinishing kit called One Stroke in 1984 that promised on its package to be "so easy a child can do it." Another part of the package warned: "Keep out of reach of children."

In what sneaky way did the Chicago mail-order firm of J. C. Whitney & Co. try to con a dollar out of unwary customers of its auto-parts catalog in 1987?

On the order form, just above the line where customers total the amount of their order, it read, "I am adding $1.00 for a full years [sic] subscription to your catalog." Only sharp-eyed consumers who carefully studied the opposite side of the order form saw a notice that said customers receive all of Whitney's catalogs free.

CUSTOMER DISSERVICE

THE CONSUMER BE DAMNED

How Chrysler Took Customers for a Ride

Chrysler hoodwinked car buyers by letting employees test-drive tens of thousands of the company's new autos with their odometers disconnected before selling the cars as new.

In June of 1987, a grand jury in St. Louis handed down a felony fraud indictment that charged Chrysler had sent more than 60,000 new cars to dealers, with no hint that employees had driven them for up to 400 miles—and, in some cases, actually damaged them.

The scandal unfolded after several Chrysler executives were caught speeding by Missouri troopers in 1986. The execs all used the same defense—the speedometer didn't work.

An investigation revealed that plant managers routinely drove new cars on personal business for up to five weeks with the speedometers and odometers disconnected. Investigators discovered that employees crashed at least forty of the cars, repaired them at Chrysler plants, and passed them off to dealers as brand new.

At first, Chrysler officials called the charges "an outrage." They claimed employees simply drove the cars home and back to sample production-line quality. They defended the practice as legal because the law on odometer fraud applies only to used cars.

But the public didn't buy that excuse. Fearing a backlash from consumers, Chrysler chairman Lee Iacocca called a press conference and did some corporate breast beating: "Did we screw up? You bet we did. We went beyond dumb and reached all the way out to stupid." He didn't stop there. Iacocca placed two-page ads in national newspapers explaining the company's error.

Chrysler pleaded no contest to the criminal charges. As part of a settlement, Chrysler extended its warranty on all 60,000 test cars for two years or 20,000 additional miles, gave $500 in cash to the owners, and promised to give forty customers whose cars were damaged during the "test-driving" new vehicles.

Teller to the Machines

No banking policy backfired as badly as the one concocted by Citibank in 1983 when it decreed that customers with balances under $5,000 would have to use automatic cash machines instead of tellers.

"We shot ourselves in the foot," admitted Richard S. Braddock, executive vice-president of the nation's second largest bank.

In an effort to increase the use of its automatic teller machines, the giant New York bank in 1981 quietly began a policy in selected branches of providing teller services only for high-deposit customers. When Citibank put tellers off limits to the nickel-and-dime crowd at one of its largest Manhattan branches in 1983, the bank was besieged by a consumer revolt.

Echoing the protests of many customers, David Greenberg, of the Consumer Federation of America, said the policy was not only offensive, but also unfair. "Automatic tellers were designed to provide consumers with convenience, not to create second-class citizens," he declared.

Among those few who were delighted with Citibank's faux pas were officials at the rival Chemical Bank of New York. To lure away angered Citibank customers, a nearby Chemical branch promoted human kindness over mechanical efficiency. Banners that said TELLERS LOVE CUSTOMERS were hung outside Chemical's branch, tellers wore "TLC" buttons, the staff served customers coffee and sweet rolls, and a mime entertained outside. Checking account openings doubled in the first two weeks of the campaign.

After two months of stinging criticism, Citibank admitted it goofed and restored every customer's privilege to choose between humans and machines. "We made a mistake in terms of how we viewed the problem," said Citibank's Braddock. "We didn't spend enough time on the issue of customer choice."

But if the lesson was that you can't treat customers differently, Citibank didn't learn it. A week after admitting its mistake, the bank created another controversy when it sought to solicit out-of-state customers by offering them a higher yield on money market accounts than it was offering to New York area customers.

Despite local consumer outrage, the bank refused to offer the better rates to New Yorkers. Only when the switchboard was jammed with hundreds of irate calls did Citibank relent. It had finally learned its lesson.

"I'M SORRY, SIR. THERE'S NO CHARGE FOR USING THE DICTAPHONE, BUT IF YOU WANT TO TALK TO A LIVE SECRETARY IT'LL COST YOU A BUCK AND A QUARTER EXTRA."

Say Goodbye to Hello

Customers have learned not to expect a chatty, informal greeting from employees at Morgan Guaranty Trust Co.

Workers at the New York bank were told to convey a blue-blooded image in their dress and conduct—and in their telephone manners.

The bank's 1983 in-house telephone directory opened with the following edict: "Avoid saying 'hello.' This elsewhere pleasant and familiar greeting is out of place in the world of business." Instead, the book instructed, "Identify yourself, such as 'bookkeeping department, Miss Smith speaking.'" Apparently, employees, if they felt customers deserved it, could say "goodbye."

How did Coleco Industries break the little hearts of millions of children?

To spur sales of Cabbage Patch Kids in 1984, Coleco promised to send first-birthday cards to the 3.2 million dolls assigned fall birthdays whose "moms" and "dads" had registered them. Unfortunately, Coleco didn't follow through, triggering a flood of tears from Patch parents.

Enlightening Customers

When General Electric discovered that in rare cases some of their lamps could explode, it responsibly sent customers a form letter warning them of the possible danger. After scaring consumers out of their wits, GE then had the audacity to tell them not to worry.

The letter, dated December 20, 1985, bore the heading: "Important Message to Users of GE Multi-Vapor and Mercury Lamps" and said in part:

"There exists the possibility with any of these lamp types, regardless of wattage, that the arc tube may unexpectedly rupture due to internal causes or external factors, such as a systems failure or misapplication. When this occurs, the glass outer jacket surrounding the arc tube could break and particles of extremely hot quartz from the arc tubes and glass fragments from the outer jacket will be discharged into the fixture enclosure and/or the surrounding environment thereby creating a risk of personal injury or fire. Users must recognize that metal halide lamps and mercury lamps are not risk-free. Few products found in industry today could claim to be totally risk-free. This does not mean, however, that such products should be considered 'unsafe.' " Right.

Steering Customers Wrong

Problem: General Motors discovers that all 1984 GM cars equipped with a 2.5-liter four-cylinder engine could experience a cracked block and loss of coolant, resulting in repairs that could cost up to $2,000 per car.

Solution: Send a secret bulletin to dealers warning them of the problem but do not mail similar notices to car owners.

Problem: The press reports the engine-block leak condition and critics blast GM for its failure to inform the owners.

Solution: GM issues a statement that says "... there's nothing secret about the policy [dealer service bulletin]. It's on file in all appropriate dealerships. Since 1983, information in each new car's glove box specifically tells customers how they can find these policies at their dealers or order them from GM. They certainly aren't secret."

Question: Speaking for all consumers, Clarence Ditlow, of the Center for Auto Safety, asks, "How can owners ask about a problem they don't know anything about, or even know exists?"

Answer: That's the beauty of GM's solution.

Ford's Quick Fix

How's this for customer service: When the owner of a new Cougar informed the Ford Motor Co. that her license plate and its holder were bent, the company immediately dispatched an engineer from Detroit to New York City to investigate.

But don't expect the same treatment. This was a classic case of high-level favoritism.

Shortly after buying her Cougar in 1981, Marian Heiskell discovered the license-plate problem and demanded action. Ford responded just as it would for any other lady who happened to be on the board of directors of both Ford and *The New York Times*.

When word of the favoritism leaked out, Ford lamely explained that it was just good business practice. After all, said a company spokesman, if Mrs. Heiskell's license plate had been bent by a defective license-plate holder, license plates all over the country might be bending. "If we could catch it early, we'd save far more than the $350 it cost to send a repairman to New York," said the spokesman.

As it turned out, it was a defective license plate that made the license-plate holder bend, not the other way around. Said the Ford man sheepishly, "I guess we overreacted somewhat."

Flying Circus

(PART ONE)
When airlines merge, customer service often nosedives.

Take, for example, what happened in February 1987 on a Continental Airlines flight from Denver to Miami. Passengers complained that dinner consisted of a cold roast beef sandwich, potato chips, and an apple. The complaints soon became too much for the chief flight attendant, who took to the intercom and confessed he was "embarrassed" about the "substandard" service.

"This is a Frontier airplane," he said. "Frontier Airlines was recently bought by People Express, which was bought by Texas Air [which also bought Continental]. Continental Airline's catering service is handling this flight, and their trays don't fit in our ovens."

Passengers were invited to send comment cards from the in-flight magazine to Texas Air executives. Five minutes later, the attendant acknowledged that none of the magazines had comment cards left, so he gave out the office address of Texas Air chairman Frank Lorenzo. Said the frustrated attendant, "He's responsible."

Flying Circus

(PART TWO)
To improve the quality of the booze in coach class in 1980, Alvin Feldman, then president of Continental Airlines, stocked up on Chivas Regal Scotch. But he didn't know what to pour in first class until he took the advice of a Beverly Hills bartender who suggested Johnny Walker Black Label.

That didn't fly too high with many first-class passengers, who glared with envy at the budget-minded folks in the aft sipping good old Chivas. To keep tempers down, flight attendants began swiping Chivas Regal from coach and smuggling it into first class.

Eventually, Chivas Regal became the official Scotch for both classes. A Continental spokesman said the airline had enough bottles of Black Label to last years.

Not Worth the Paper They're Printed On

Ludens Inc.'s 5th Avenue candy bar carries a nutty "guarantee of satisfaction" on its wrapper. If you're not completely satisfied, just mail the uneaten portion of the 50-cent candy bar (which will cost you 39 cents postage) along with an explanation of your dissatisfaction to Ludens. You won't get your money back. Instead, the company will send you *another* 5th Avenue. And what if you don't like that one? Ludens will send you another . . .

Unisonic Products Corp. requires a steady hand or a magnifying glass to fill out the warranty for its Unisonic calculator. The warranty is a postcard only 2 inches wide and 3⅝ inches long! You're supposed to send in the warranty right away. But it's unlikely that the warranty will ever reach its destination—unless it's put in an envelope—because postal regulations prohibit the mailing of a postcard less than 3½ inches by 5 inches.

Sharp says that if its cheapest quartz watch needs repairing under its one-year warranty, you must pay a $4.95 handling charge (plus postage for shipping to the factory). The watch itself only costs $2.97.

Saikosha America offers an impressive warranty on its bicycle lock. The company says it will pay up to $350 if, within a year, the lock is forced open and the bicycle is stolen. However, among the things you must do to validate the warranty is to provide a copy of the sales receipt for the *bike* or a signed, dated appraisal from a bicycle dealer. Not only that, but the bike has to be registered with the local police department.

Wolter Inc., maker of water heaters for boats, pledges a money-back guarantee. If, within thirty days, you're not completely satisfied, you can get a refund by returning the product "unused and uninstalled."

Cable Electric Products has a simple warranty to fill out on its Snapit 6+2=8 multi-outlet system. Just complete and mail the registration form and retain the warranty. So what's the hitch? The warranty is on the back of the registration form.

> WHY PEOPLE STUFF MONEY IN MATTRESSES
>
> The National Bank of Detroit sent a letter to its customers in 1985 informing them that its "24 Hour Banker machines" would be open less than eight hours a day.
>
> Planters Bank in Memphis charged customers $1 for the privilege of waiting in line to talk to a live teller.
>
> Manufacturers Hanover Trust Co. set up a special express "priority line" at its New York branches in 1984 for depositors with $25,000 in the bank. The less affluent were charged $1.50 to enjoy the same benefits of life in the fast lane.

Phoney Charges

(EXHIBIT NO. 1)
Rather than give a rate card for long-distance charges, the Dupont Plaza Hotel in Washington, D.C., placed the following notice in its rooms in 1985: "Through the use of new technology, hotels are now able to reduce guests' long-distance phone bills ... To defray the additional expense for this new system, a 75-cent charge per call and 75 cents for each operator-assisted long-distance call will be added to your bill."

(EXHIBIT NO. 2)
Pacific Bell sent a letter to its customers in 1987 stating that if they subscribe to the company's "Per-Month Wire Repair Plan" for only 50 cents per month, they can continue to receive service calls for inside wiring "at no extra charge."

Thank You for Being Such Good Customers— That Will Be $45,000, Please

First, the Good News: Iowa Power & Light Co. sent letters to 113,000 of its residential customers in 1987, thanking them for paying their bills on time. The gesture, said the Des Moines utility, was part of a campaign to become more "customer focused."

Now, the Not-So-Good News: Guess who's going to pay the $45,000 tab for sending those thank-you letters? The utility announced its intentions to include the cost of the mailing the next time it asked for a rate increase.

We'll Make You an Offer You Can Refuse

Valvoline Oil Co. offered a $2.40 rebate in 1985 with a purchase of twelve quarts of motor oil. To collect, consumers had to send in a dated sales receipt for the twelve cans, plus the emblems from seven cans—all within thirty days of purchase. Unfortunately, consumers often cut too deeply into the can to remove the emblem and the oil leaked out. And, to top it all, most cars required no more than five quarts for an oil change.

Flavor Tree put a label on the jar of its Sesame Crunch snack treat in 1984 declaring, "Free Trial Offer Inside." Only after eating most of the snack was the small coupon found at the bottom. The coupon stated that to receive a refund of the purchase price, the consumer had to send in the inner seal from the jar, the cash-register tape, and the coupon. But by the time the coupon was found, the typical buyer had long since thrown out the inner seal, not to mention the cash-register tape.

Salada Foods Inc. teed off consumers with a misleading refund in 1986. The box of tea bags included a sticker that promised a $1 refund, with "details on the back of the sticker." Purchasers had to open the box to read the back of the sticker—which gave them the grating news that they had to buy two boxes to get the refund.

Mott's USA enticed consumers in 1986 with the promise of a free carton of juice with proof of purchase of a carton of its apple-grape juice. Once they bought it, buyers were able to read the inside of the carton, which revealed Mott's definition of proof of purchase—the price codes from five packs of juice.

Procter & Gamble had consumers scrambling for their atlases. The company offered a complete refund on the purchase price of Secret deodorant in 1985. All the buyer had to do was mail in the cash-register tape and proof of purchase to: "Secret Purchase Price Refund, P.O. Box 7244, TBD." Anyone know where TBD is?

Hanes Hosiery hosed plenty of women in 1986 with its promise on the package of Summeralls panty hose of a "$5.00 cash refund." The refund label stated "purchase proofs required—see details inside." The details inside stated that proofs of purchase were needed all right—but for other types of Hanes panty hose, not for Summeralls.

IMPERSONNEL RELATIONS

COMPANY MISTREATMENT OF ITS EMPLOYEES

Bonus of Contention

Why was General Motors' 1982 bonus plan—which included generous increases in executive compensation, more executive stock options, and lucrative bonus money for top managers—so incredibly ill-timed?

The bonus-plan announcement hit the streets on the very day General Motors and the United Auto Workers were to sign an agreement calling for "necessary" wage concessions to save the company. The union was so furious it forced GM to postpone the implementation of the bonus plan for the life of the thirty-month labor contract. Said the *Automotive News,* "The company could not have done more to infuriate the rank and file of its work force if it had set out to do just that."

Is This Any Way to Treat Employees?

Giant retailer W. T. Grant, which went bankrupt in 1975, made it a practice to cut the tie of any sales manager who did not meet his quota.

Ben Love, chairman and CEO of Texas Commerce Bancshares, issued a fourteen-page memo on appropriate attire for his employees in 1985. Banned were fitted European suits, plaids—"if you can recognize the pattern from across the room"—and, for women, fake jewelry.

"I WAS HERE A YEAR BEFORE I REALIZED THAT, JUST BY SLUFFING OFF A BIT, I COULD GET RID OF MY MOTHER-IN-LAW'S CHRISTMAS GIFTS WITH NO GUILT ATTACHED."

The Miller Brewing Co. has locked its doors at 8:00 A.M., making managers identify themselves to gain access. It then sent them "Nastygrams" when they were late.

Public Service Electric & Gas Co., of Newark, New Jersey, acted like Big Brother in 1981–82 by monitoring more than just customer calls to its service representatives. When the employees hung up the phone, company listening devices kept right on recording all their other in-office conversations.

A Turkey of an Employer?

For several years, going to the rest room was easier for grade-schoolers than it was for the employees at the world's largest turkey processor.

In 1984, that was one of the main reasons workers of the United Food and Commercial Workers Local 400 went on a three-year strike against Rocco Enterprises, a Virginia food conglomerate.

Management conducted a study of "unscheduled" bathroom use of production-line workers. The firm calculated that at four to six minutes per trip, employees were spending a total of 281.1 hours in the rest rooms each year. Foremen were instructed to supervise a tightly controlled bathroom pass system—but that wound up using 147 hours of supervisory time, according to the union. Meanwhile, the workers were frequently unable to leave the line when necessary, causing an occasional embarrassment.

"They don't have time to let you go to the bathroom, but they have a half hour's time to write you up in the office," complained one worker.

Added another disgruntled employee, "Sometimes you have to wait an hour to go to the bathroom after getting permission from the foreman. Then you have to carry a pass. My child at school can go to the rest room easier than I can—and I'm an adult."

What company has treated its workers with such consistency that they have gone out on strike every three years since 1968?

Phelps Dodge, at its copper mines in Morenci, Arizona.

Raked over the Coals

Barrie Bergman called on fire and brimstone to motivate his employees.

He had them walk over hot coals barefoot!

Bergman, who heads Record Bar Inc., the nation's second-largest retailer of records and tapes, persuaded hundreds of his workers to bare their soles and tread across six-foot-long beds of glowing-red coals during a seminar in 1985. It was part of the company's "human systems" program for developing employees' potential to their fullest. "Firewalking is a metaphor for no limits," Bergman explained.

According to *The Wall Street Journal,* Record Bar workers who didn't have a burning desire to walk across hot coals were encouraged to leave the Durham, North Carolina–based company. "I feel very strongly about our program," Bergman told the *Journal.* "If employees don't like what we're doing, then they should go someplace else."

According to Bergman, this bizarre management training session was designed to generate innovative business ideas and increase sales.

Will it only be a matter of time before the following scene takes place? A Record Bar manager calls in a low-achieving salesman, rakes him over the coals, and tells him, "Your sales are abysmal, Jones. Go take a firewalk."

Why should you never tell a joke to an employee during working hours at the Shropshire, England, plant of Tatung—a manufacturer of the Einstein personal microcomputer?

The high-tech computer company has banned employees from laughing while on the job.

"THAT'S A FRIGHTFULLY AMUSING STORY, PEARSON. SHALL WE MEET IN THE PUB AFTER WORK SO I CAN BLOODY WELL SPLIT A GUT LAUGHING AT IT?..."

Cola War Casualties

The biggest enemy Coca-Cola faces in its war with rival Pepsi is itself. Coke's paranoia has cost the jobs of several loyal employees.

Victim No. 1: In the summer of 1985, a Coca-Cola bottler in

Oxford, Alabama, suspended an employee for three days for drinking Pepsi at Burger King during working hours. But a Pepsi bottler in Birmingham took care of the suspended Coke employee—by sending him a check to cover his lost wages.

Victim No. 2: In 1985, Amanda Blake was fired from her job as manager of data processing at the Coke bottler in Northampton, Massachusetts—because she refused to break her engagement with David Cronin, an accountant at a rival Pepsi bottler. Apparently, love has no place in Coke's business world. Its attorney justified the sacking by claiming if Amanda stayed, she could have inadvertently leaked confidential information to the man she loved.

Victim No. 3: Michael Wilson lost his job as a Coke deliveryman in Shelbyville, Indiana, after he won a free trip in a contest sponsored by Pepsi. In March 1987, Wilson found a winning Pepsi bottle cap that earned him a free trip to New Orleans for the college basketball championship. Because Wilson was a die-hard fan of the Indiana University Hoosiers—who were in the finals—nothing was going to keep him from attending. When his bosses "strongly advised" him to turn down the trip, Wilson refused and quickly found himself out of a job. However, Pepsi came to his rescue. James Rogers, area vice-president for Pepsi in Indianapolis, wrote Wilson: "You know, Mike, sometimes even the cola wars play second string, and Hoosier hysteria is one of those times. Next week, after IU wins the championship [it did, too], we go back at it in the cola wars. This time, we want you on our team." Rogers said he offered Wilson the job because "when it comes to the love of Indiana basketball, nothing should stand in the way."

How to Drive Workers Mad

Richard Moe, chairman of *Delta Rubber Co.,* banned Japanese cars from the company parking lot in 1983 because he blamed Japanese imports for a $3 million drop in sales of the firm's wiper blades and rubber ball-bearing seals.

"I can't tell you how to spend your money," he told workers in a memo, "but I certainly don't have to provide you [owners of Japanese cars] with a parking place." Even visitors with Japanese cars were shunned. A sign near the company's parking lot ordered them to park their cars across the street—next to the backstop of a Little League field.

When Stanley Pace, president of *TRW*, was named chairman of United Way's Cleveland-area fund drive in 1984, plant officials tried to impress the boss by using strong-arm tactics in the company parking lot.

To produce record contributions for Pace, the managers assigned United Way contributors parking spaces closest to the plant. New parking regulations were issued that included a threat to fire noncontributors who parked in contributors' spaces. The plant's union had a name for this type of charity squeeze—"extortion."

In 1984, the *Ford Motor Co.* began requiring employees at its engine plant in Lima, Ohio, to park in a back lot more than a half mile away from the factory if they drove foreign cars.

Howard Fields, fifty-six, who had worked at the plant for twenty-eight years, ignored the new rule and continued to leave his 1981 Nissan in the front lot. His car was plastered with plastic warning stickers and twice towed away. Then things got rough. Over a three-month period, Ford suspended Fields seven times. As if that wasn't punishment enough, Ford then fired him.

St. Mary's Paper Inc. in Ontario should have put up this sign in its paper plant—it had forbidden employees to read anything from current events to classics during their breaks.

In fact, the only thing the company allowed its workers to read was material on the pulp and paper industry.

In a 1986 memo to its 460 employees, the plant's management said it wanted to instill a "new work ethic" by restricting break activities. "We feel the reading of newspapers, paperbacks, and card playing isn't conducive to the success of our operation," said the memo.

When questioned about the ridiculously strict ban, a company spokesman said that workers had a broad selection of reading materials available at several library stalls. Imagine the enjoyment employees received browsing through pamphlets on wrapping paper, the intellectual stimulus they got reading about grinding pulp, or the emotional rush they felt after perusing booklets on slashing logs.

The local Canadian Paperworks Union protested the policy by refusing to read anything during their breaks. The company finally got the message and lifted the ban on books.

Rolls-Royce Motors Inc. terminated its franchise agreement with Charles Schmitt in 1985 even though the St. Louis dealer sold more Rolls-Royces and Bentleys than anyone else in America. Was it because:

A. He was a flamboyant bachelor whose love for the nightlife irritated blue-blood Rolls-Royce executives.
B. Rolls Royce dumped him to mollify its other U.S. dealers who were jealous of his success.
C. Rolls Royce didn't think Schmitt's high-volume, low-price sales style fit its image.
D. All of the above.

Answer: D

Thanks but No Thanks

How did Citicorp employees respond when William Spencer, president of the big New York bank holding company, told them in 1980 they wouldn't get their usual 10–15 percent end-of-year incentive-plan bonus?

By sending the following memo to Spencer and Citicorp chairman Walter Wriston. The staff memo thanked them both:

"... for showing your appreciation to those of us who, in 1980 during the transit strike, woke up in the middle of the night, spending hours walking over bridges and through tunnels, riding bikes and thumbing rides . . . to get to work at Citibank at the crack of dawn.

". . . for the fair salaries we receive, as you raise your lending rates, and food and rent prices rise.

". . . for all your automation, making many jobs obsolete, and for those of us who still have jobs, making them harder, due to system delays and/or system failures.

". . . for letting us share in the honor and glory, but not the profits, of working for the No. 1 bank.

". . . for our inspiring slogan for 1981, 'Service Is a Word—You Make It Work.' For all your words of wisdom and memos through 1980, we, too, have a slogan: 'Incentive Is Just a Word—YOU Make It Work.' Unfortunately, man does not survive by words."

Why did Pan Am's distrust of flight attendants prove so costly?

Convinced that flight attendants were stealing 35-cent miniature liquor bottles on flights, Pan Am security personnel rigged a clock device to the liquor cabinet to record the times of the alleged thefts. While airborne, a flight attendant heard the ticking and thought there was a bomb aboard. The captain rerouted the plane to the nearest airport, where passengers were evacuated by emergency exits. The unscheduled landing cost Pan Am $15,000. The airline never did find any evidence of thievery.

Striking Back

In one of the most bizarre episodes in labor relations, a company sued a union because the union *didn't* go on strike.

In 1983, Colonial Manor Nursing Home of Youngstown, Ohio, took the Service Employees International Union to court for not following through on the union's threat to strike.

When labor negotiations between the workers and the nursing home broke down, union members authorized a strike and gave Colonial a ten-day notice of their intentions as required by federal law.

The nursing home responded by spending $15,000 to recruit, interview, and train people to fill the forty-seven jobs it expected to be vacant from the anticipated strike. However, the union didn't go on strike. On the day the strike was supposed to begin, the union employees showed up for work—and so did the replacements.

Faced with meeting the payroll for two staffs, Colonial sued the union for "fraud and negligence" and asked for $3 million in punitive damages in addition to actual damages. The union countersued. Eventually, both sides settled their dispute at the bargaining table and dropped their lawsuits.

Out of a Jobs

Steven Jobs was hailed as the embodiment of Silicon Valley's entrepreneurial spirit after he cofounded Apple Computer Inc. in 1977.

So how did the company that he started reward him? It unceremoniously ousted him—an action taken by the very professional manager that Jobs had handpicked.

Apple president John Sculley, whom Jobs personally brought into the company, forced Jobs out of his operating position as head of the Macintosh division in 1985. Jobs was exiled to a building across the street from Apple headquarters that he and his secretary called "Siberia."

As further humiliation, the company gave Jobs the ridiculously worthless title of "global visionary" and had little or nothing for him to do. Out of frustration, Jobs resigned as chairman of the board. "I mean, in my wildest imagination, I couldn't have come up with such a wild ending to all of this," he lamented to the press.

Merry Christmas, You're Fired

If you're going to follow in the footsteps of an entrepreneur, why not choose Ebenezer Scrooge?

That's what the New York outplacement firm of Bushnell, Cruise & Associates did during the holiday season in 1984 when it sent out press releases claiming that the best time to fire someone is at Christmas and Hanukkah.

In a release entitled "Holidays Good Time for Job Hunting," the company said that executives shouldn't let themselves be overcome by "well-intentioned sympathy." If you're going to bounce someone, do it during the holiday season because that's the "perfect time [for fired employees] to reach out to people, to meet old friends, and to spread the word that they're available," said Paul Cruise, president of the firm.

Bushnell Cruise didn't give this advice out of the goodness—or badness—of its heart. "Our slowest time, without doubt, is from mid-December to early January," said the release.

"IN ADDITION TO THE TRADITIONAL REDS AND GREENS, YOU'LL NOTICE THAT OUR LITTLE OFFICE TREE HAS A MORE CONTEMPORARY COLOR-TONE THIS YEAR... PINK SLIPS."

Hats Off to Management

Just days before Christmas, 1987, 23 workers of the Okonite Co. decided to add a little joy to their world by wearing Santa Claus caps at work.

But to management, it was not the season to be jolly. When employees donned their gay apparel, they were promptly suspended for three days because, management claimed, the holiday hats were "not appropriate for a business environment."

The following day, about 100 more employees—nearly half the work force of the electrical cable manufacturer—put on the Christmas head gear. They too were suspended by their unbending employer, who threatened to fire any worker who continued to wear the red hats with white trim.

Workers said the company had no regulation against wearing hats on the job, and that most of them had worn baseball caps without incident. "I wear a hat the whole year in here, and this is the only hat I'm suspended for," worker Ed Reilly complained to the press.

At a protest rally outside the North Brunswick, New Jersey, plant, the suspended workers wore their Santa Claus caps and sang "Jingle Bells." Then they returned to work—without their holiday hats.

Why did employees at the Chrysler Proving Ground feel they were being treated like schoolchildren in 1974?

When two workers were caught drag racing on Chrysler's big oval test track, their supervisor suspended them for one day and made each of them write a 2,000-word essay on "Why I Should Not Be Caught Drag Racing at the Proving Ground."

THE RANK AND VILE

INCOMPETENCE IN THE WORK FORCE

You Just Can't Get Good Help These Days

Imagine the surprise when shoppers opened the 1982 Montgomery Ward catalog and found a *Playboy* centerfold in the middle. A Montgomery Ward spokesman said the catalog and the magazine were printed in the same shop, and, as "an employee prank," the centerfold was stapled into a few catalogs.

Thousands of Lawrence Welk fans who bought his album *Polka Party* had their ears burned in 1987. The record contained the punk rock soundtrack to *Sid and Nancy,* a movie about former Sex Pistols member Sid Vicious who allegedly killed his girlfriend before he died of a heroin overdose. About 10,000 albums "apparently were mislabeled at the factory," said Bernice McGeehan of the Welk Music Group. "We got several telephone calls from ladies who said they were shocked by the language on the record. They said they couldn't even repeat it."

Part of the fun of eating Cracker Jack is the prize in the box. But John Iglesias of Santa Ana, California, was shocked when he pulled out a miniature sex manual from a box of the snack treat in 1983. Said a stunned Iglesias, "I was thinking it was going to be little pages of cartoons or little paste-on tattoos." Borden, Inc., manufacturer of Cracker Jack, claimed it had instituted "extensive security measures" to thwart any other budding Dr. Ruths.

Among the tons of paper thrown from office buildings during a New York ticker-tape parade for the 1984 Olympic medal winners were hundreds of listings of Bear, Stearns & Co.'s client accounts and transactions. Dozens of competing pinstriped brokers scrambled around the street and sidewalk snatching up customer leads. One broker walked away with 100 sheets listing Bear Stearns accounts, complete with names, addresses, dollar volume, and portfolio details. "Frankly, we are embarrassed," Bear Stearns managing partner Alvin Einbender told the press. "I haven't caught the person who did it, but if I did and we were an Islamic country, we would probably punish him suitably."

When relations between the unions and Revlon had reached an all-time low in 1947, angry workers found a novel way to display their disgust for the company. The workers who assembled makeup compacts began slipping notes in them that read, "Fuck you."

During labor unrest with Ford and General Motors in the 1960s, assembly-line workers occasionally would toss a loose bolt into the deep recesses of the companies' most expensive cars—the Cadillac and Lincoln Continental. The rattle drove owners nuts.

Lost and Found in the Banking World

Lost: 8,000 checks worth $894,000
From: First Security Bank of Idaho in Boise, July 1971
Found: Shredded in garbage bags

Six boxes of cleared checks drawn on other banks and deposited by First Security Bank customers were left on the floor for the night. A janitor, subbing for the regular one who was on vacation, thought they were old checks that needed to be shredded. So that's what he did.

When bank officials arrived the next morning, they couldn't find the checks. At 12:30 P.M. they finally located the checks—or what was left of them—in the alley in two huge plastic sacks.

"The checks looked like confetti," recalled Dave Eiguren, bank vice-president. "We decided to pull them out of the sacks in handfuls and tape them back together. So we hired ninety part-time workers and it took them six weeks to finish the job."

Lost: Thousands of checks worth $227 million
From: Continental Illinois Bank of Chicago, August 1986
Found: In trash heap next to compacting machine

To the weekend cleaning woman at Continental Illinois, the plastic bags on the floor of the computer room looked like trash. So she threw them onto a garbage heap along with the dirty coffee cups and other office detritus for the compacting machine.

But the following Monday, Continental's data processors discovered they were short $227 million in checks that the bank had honored but had not yet entered in its computers. An in-house all-points-bulletin was issued as a crew of janitors, clerks, and even managers began sifting through the smelly trash in the garbage room. The dirty work finally paid off. After a few hours of searching, the checks were rescued from the dumpster.

If the checks had not been found, Continental would have faced the laborious task of straightening out nearly a quarter-billion-dollar imbalance in its books.

What was the "employee attitude problem" at Philadelphia Electric Co.'s Peach Bottom nuclear power plant that caused the Nuclear Regulatory Commission to close it in 1987?

The control-room operators had been caught napping and playing video games on the night shift.

> Listing in 1980 Atlanta Yellow Pages under heading "Men's Clothing & Furnishings, Retail":
>
> Bank Joseph A Clothiers Inc.
> 3384 Peachtree Rd NE 262-7100
>
> Listing in 1981 Atlanta Yellow Pages after same store called and asked Southern Bell Telephone Co. to "drop 'Inc.' ":
>
> Drop Inc
> 3384 Peachtree Rd NE 262-7100

Kill the Messenger

Thousands of business messages are transmitted every day without incident. But on rare occasions, the signals get crossed—and so do the senders.

WESTERN UNION

In 1981, Gene Milner, the earthy chairman of Lanier Business Products Inc., decided to fire up his sales force with a Mailgram. Western Union sent his message out not only to the salesmen, but inadvertently to another audience—500 Catholic school principals, many of whom were priests and nuns.

Imagine how perplexed they were when they received Milner's Mailgram, which said, "I am counting on your tails being out there in the field selling for the rest of this month and all of May. I don't want to hear nothing but that you are producing. Don't hire—don't do nothing else. Don't fiddle with papers. Don't talk on the phone to your grandmother. Get the hell busy for the rest of the fiscal year."

The next day several indignant priests and nuns telephoned Milner, demanding to know exactly what he meant by that message. Milner then sent another Mailgram apologizing to the principals. It's not known if Western Union sent a Mailgram apologizing to Milner.

GRAPHIC SCANNING CORP.

In December 1984, the securities firm of L. F. Rothschild, Unterberg, Towbin sent wires to other underwriters announcing it had been sued and reminded them that they were required to pay their share of the legal costs. The messages were transmitted for the firm by Graphic Scanning Corp., which then took it upon itself to end each somber wire with "Happy Holidays." A Graphic spokesman said the season's greetings were sincere, but he lamented the "unfortunate juxtaposition."

WOODHOUSE DRAKE & CAREY INC.

As one of the largest international sugar dealers, Woodhouse sent a top-secret in-house memo to several dozen customers by mistake.

The memo, transmitted by a company official in New York to the London office in March 1984, was then inadvertently included in a telex from London to customers. It contained highly unflattering remarks about competitors and detailed information on trading strategies. Within days, nearly half of all U.S. sugar dealers had a bootlegged copy of the memo. They took advantage of it to cut into Woodhouse's market and shake up the entire industry.

Costly Dividends

Why was Manufacturers Hanover Trust Co. so upset after it sent a quarterly common-stock dividend to shareholders of American Home Products Corp. in 1979?

The bank accidentally mailed about $7.8 million too much to about 78,000 stockholders. When the bank discovered it had added an extra five cents a share, horrified executives rushed out thousands of Mailgrams and letters to the recipients, pleading for understanding—and the excess money. They got almost all of it back—at a cost of $33,000 in extra postage and $7,000 in extra labor.

Why did it seem that the Cleveland bank holding company AmeriTrust was owned and run by *retired* chairman M. Brock Weir in 1983?

When a bank employee was instructed to change the addresses of Weir's many personal AmeriTrust accounts, the clerk also changed the address of the corporate checking account. Statements of the Cleveland company, which had assets of $5.8 billion, were sent 1,300 miles away to Weir's new home in Sebastopol, California.

Net Loss in Confidence
How Four Companies Shook Customer Faith

Dominion Securities Pitfield Ltd., Canada's largest securities dealer, recommended that its clients sell shares of Datagram Inc., a small Montreal maker of data communications equipment. The brokers had read an item on the Dow Jones News Service that they believed reported a loss for the company. Following Dominion's advice, many clients sold their Datagram stock only to see it climb 40 percent the following week. What angered them even more was that Dominion's brokers misread the news account, which referred not to Data*gram*, but to Data*ram*, a New Jersey–based maker of computer memories.

How did the Neenah Foundry, of Neenah, Wisconsin, spell trouble for one of its customers—the City of Fayetteville, Arkansas—in 1987?

The foundry made 197 manhole covers for the city—and misspelled the town's name on every one of them. The covers were all spelled "Fayettville," without a middle "e." After offering the city a 25 percent discount, which was rejected, the foundry reluctantly agreed to take back the covers and recast them. According to city officials, a foundry salesman misspelled the name on his order. That salesman no longer works for the foundry.

Prudential-Bache Securities showed clients a split personality. As co-writer of the 50-million-share public offering of Continental Illinois Corp. stock in the fall of 1986, Pru-Bache had its sales force talk up the stock to investors. It suggested a price of $6.25 a share. But a few months later, with the stock selling at $5.75, Pru-Bache's top bank analysts pronounced Continental's stock as "overvalued." The announcement came after Pru-Bache sold its portion of the offered shares for a $1.2 million profit.

Manufacturers Hanover Trust Co. took out newspaper ads in 1980 notifying owners of unclaimed assets that they had money on account. Manny Hanny's customers questioned the bank's intelligence when the ad listed the following account holders, among others, as having an "address unknown": Dow Jones & Co., New York Telephone Co., the Internal Revenue Service, Bank of America, Morgan Guaranty Trust Co., and Mitsubishi Motor Corp.

Moody's Investors Service reported in May 1984 that it was upgrading its debt rating of Cole National Corp., a specialty retailer based in Cleveland. Moody's said it was impressed by the company's Circus World toy-store division, which, Moody's added, gave Cole its "largest portion of sales and profits." However, Cole never owned Circus World. Its competitor, Rite Aid, a drugstore chain, owned it.

Why did the ad folks at J. Walter Thompson nearly gag when Coca-Cola was served during a celebration of the opening of their new Manhattan offices in 1981?

Thompson held the accounts for Pepsico Inc.'s Teem; Coke's advertising agency was McCann-Erickson. After a firm word from Thompson executives, Pepsi became the exclusive cola of the evening.

FUNNY BUSINESS

ZAPPING THE COMPETITION

Beer Wars

MILLER BREWING VS. ANHEUSER-BUSCH

A-B's First Salvo: A-B complains to the Federal Trade Commission in 1977 that Miller's premium beer, Lowenbrau, is marketed as a German beer of the same name brewed since the fourteenth century. But, says A-B, Miller merely bought rights to use the name in the U.S. for a beer brewed by modern methods in Texas. The FTC orders Miller to change its advertising to reflect that Lowenbrau is not the German product.

Miller's Retaliation: Miller declares war on A-B by announcing, "We find it incredulous [sic] that the world's largest brewer would ask the FTC to protect them. It seems apparent that the crown on the King of Beers is slipping."

Miller's Next Attack: Miller then turns to the FTC in 1979 and complains that A-B's Natural Light beer is not natural at all but contains tannic acid and other chemicals. A press release claims that A-B's use of the word "natural" is deceptive and "corrupts the word's proper usage."

A-B's Counterattack: A-B announces that Miller is also "a chemical brewer" and forces Miller to admit it uses various chemical additives in Miller Lite.

Miller's Next Attack: Miller complains to the Bureau of Alcohol, Tobacco and Firearms that A-B's Michelob Light is "simply watered-down Michelob" made by diluting regular Michelob with carbonated water.

A-B's Retaliation: A-B tells the press Michelob Light "is an all-natural beer, and unlike Miller Lite, doesn't contain any fungal enzyme or artificial foam enhancer."

Miller's Counterattack: Miller alleges Budweiser's famous beechwood aging process consists "of dumping chemically treated lumber into a glass-lined or stainless-steel beer storage tank."

Miller's Next Attack: Miller's president, John Murphy (right), makes it known that when he gets to work in the morning, he wipes his feet on a rug imprinted with the Budweiser logo. He also displays on his desk a four-inch voodoo doll that he named after August Busch III, head of A-B.

A-B's Counterattack: When August Busch III (left) hears about the voodoo doll, he makes one of his own with red hair and ships it off to the redheaded Murphy. The doll comes with Busch's monogrammed stickpin protruding from its chest.

Miller's Retaliation: Murphy registers a new beer trademark called "Gussie," the well-known nickname of August Busch II.

Reading Up on the Competition

Robert L. Crandall, chairman of American Airlines, has been a bit obsessive about his competitors. In fact, he has bought up tens of thousands of copies of books and magazine reprints about them.

In 1984, Crandall purchased 25,000 copies of a book about Braniff International Corp. But it wasn't because he enjoyed it. The opposite was true. Crandall didn't like the way he or his airline was portrayed in it. So under his direction, American paid the publisher $150,000 to discard the books and publish a slightly reworded edition.

Then, in 1987, Crandall was at it again. This time he turned his attention to a scathing article in *Texas Monthly* about Frank Lorenzo, chairman of archrival Texas Air Corp., the nation's largest carrier. Crandall loved the dirt in the story so much that he bought 15,000 reprints to distribute at employee meetings.

What Crandall found "absolutely outstanding" about the article were such nuggets as Lorenzo's college nickname—"Frankie Smooth Talk"—and the revelation that he resigned a dorm council post at Columbia University after he and others allegedly tried to rig a student election.

Promo Wars

BATTLE OF THE BLIMPS

Blimps have conducted slow-motion dogfights in a marketing war between the world's two largest film companies.

The sky war between Eastman Kodak Co. and Fuji Photo Film Co. began in 1984 when the Japanese concern paid $7 million to outbid Kodak and become the official film of the 1984 Olympics in Los Angeles. Holding only 10 percent of the U.S. market compared to Kodak's 82 percent, Fuji basked in the glory of flying its green blimp over the Olympic grounds in its competitor's homeland.

The American company then decided to make a strategic drive into the Japanese market, where it owned a 13 percent share against Fuji's 71 percent. Spearheading the attack was Kodak's yellow and red blimp.

On August 25, 1986, Fuji executives looked out the window of their Tokyo headquarters and, to their rage, saw their archrival's blimp hovering overhead. To fend off the American invader, Fuji called its blimp back from a tour of duty in Europe. Then came the biggest blimp skirmish of the marketing conflict.

During a November 1986 weekend, the blimps maneuvered over neighboring sporting events in Tokyo. Kodak was sponsoring a judo tournament within earshot of the baseball stadium where Fuji was sponsoring a series of games between Japanese and American all-stars. A Fuji spokesman complained that the Kodak blimp came dangerously close to Fuji's airship, tried to steal the show above the crowded ballpark, and ignored requests from the Fuji pilot to retreat. A Kodak spokesman charged that the Fuji blimp violated airship regulations and was engaged in a "nasty ... hit-and-run operation."

Weeks later, Fuji was attacked from another flank—by Goodyear Tire & Rubber Co., which filed suit against the photo company for trademark infringement. The suit was settled and Goodyear is keeping a wary eye on the blimps used by Kodak, McDonald's, and Resorts International.

THE BILLBOARD WAR

Frontier Airlines and Continental Airlines took their fare wars to a Denver billboard in 1986.

A Frontier billboard just outside the city's airport promised that the carrier would "change this board" if anyone undercut Frontier's fares. When a new ticket policy at Frontier left Continental with lower fares for fourteen days, several Continental executives promptly set up camp beneath the billboard. They erected a tent atop a rented bus and strung out a thirty-foot banner telling Frontier, WE'LL BE HERE UNTIL YOU TELL THE TRUTH.

Continental further antagonized its rival by offering free meals at its ticket counters to Frontier passengers to point out that Continental didn't charge passengers extra for meals. Then it announced it was giving free sodas to Frontier pilots, saying it felt sorry for them because they had to pay 50 cents for a soda on their own flights.

Frontier sought a truce by sending some free snack boxes—for which it charged passengers $3—to the enemy camp beneath the billboard. But the Continental campers decided to bite the hand that fed them. They had the contents of one of the boxes analyzed and announced the value was only $1.26.

It Was a Stinking Job, but Someone Had to Do It

The term "corporate raiders" took on a new meaning when some overzealous sales people were caught rummaging through the garbage of a competitor.

In a sneaky ploy to obtain a rival's customer lists, bumbling employees from Advance Machine Co. plundered a dumpster belonging to Tennant Co. Both are Minneapolis makers of floor maintenance products.

The Advance men were sifting through the garbage outside Tennant's San Leandro, California, sales office in 1978 and 1979 in violation of state law before they were caught.

Tennant sued and the Minnesota Court of Appeals upheld a jury's award of $500,000. In its ruling, the court said that Advance executives knew about the scavengers but didn't reprimand them, setting a poor ethical standard.

What was so eye-opening about the way PepsiCo Inc. sued Wendy's International Inc. when the fast-food chain decided to switch from Pepsi to Coke in 1986?

Pepsi's representatives served Wendy's executives notice of the suit at their homes—between midnight and 3:00 A.M.

DOUBLE STANDARD BEARERS

CORPORATE HYPOCRISY

And to the Republic for Which It Stands . . .

For years, Republic Steel Corp. spoke out against unfair foreign competition. It promoted a "Buy American" campaign and distributed bumper stickers that read, "Thanks for buying an American car."

When Republic held a dedication ceremony in 1983 for its new $100 million plant in Cleveland, the company used a "Buy American" theme. Executives and politicians flocked to the podium to denounce foreign imports. They marveled at the highly automated plant, the equipment, and the technology designed to help Republic compete with foreign rivals in the marketplace for high-quality steel.

What wasn't mentioned was where most of that innovative equipment and engineering came from. It sure wasn't the good ol' U.S. of A. The plant was built from a German design with Japanese modifications and most of the equipment was purchased in Sweden and West Germany. Altogether, Republic admitted, only 35 percent of the plant's equipment was American-made.

"We could have gotten an American company to make it [the equipment] for us from foreign plans," a Republic vice-president told *The Wall Street Journal*. "But we wanted the best equipment we could get."

Why do some people question Chrysler chairman Lee Iacocca's sincerity when he urges everybody to "buy American"?

Iacocca appeared in print ads for Don Diego cigars, which are made in the Dominican Republic.

What's Good for the Goose . . .

Among its hundreds of recommendations on how the federal government could become more efficient, the Grace Commission urged officials to be more aggressive about collecting money owed to the government.

In his report, J. Peter Grace, head of the commission and chairman of W. R. Grace & Co., wrote, "If someone owed you a large amount of money, you probably would make quite a few attempts to get it back. Not the federal government."

The fact is the federal government has tried to collect money from corporate delinquents—including a company almost half owned by none other than W. R. Grace & Co. In 1983, the Department of Interior sued Rapoca Energy Co., one of Grace's mining firms, claiming the company owed nearly $300,000 plus interest in land reclamation fees.

It Depends on Where You're Sitting

Alvin Feldman's view of a proposed 1979 merger between Continental Airlines and Western Airlines from his seat as president of rival Frontier Airlines:

The merger would violate antitrust laws and reduce competition. Any benefits would be "paltry rather than significant." (Accepting the arguments of Feldman's airline, the Civil Aeronautics Board blocked the merger.)

Alvin Feldman's view of a proposed 1981 merger between Continental Airlines and Western Airlines from his seat as the new president of Continental:

The merger would benefit passengers and strengthen the airline industry. (How did the proposed merger—which the CAB once again rejected—become so much more beneficial after two years? "As you get older," Feldman said, "you get smarter.")

Those Who Can't Do, Teach

Continental Illinois Bank—whose bad loans brought it to the brink of bankruptcy in 1984 before it was saved by the largest federal government bail-out of a private company—thought it should help others.

While it was trying to survive financially, the bank distributed a self-help manual to high school students titled, "How Will You Manage Your Money?" Surely not the Continental Illinois way.

Do As I Say, Not As I Do

In the early 1980s, Baldwin-United Corp. was one of the nation's biggest sellers of liability insurance for directors of corporations.

But the firm never spread the message to one important group—its own directors. Lacking liability insurance, Baldwin-United's directors became—much to their chagrin—a perfect example of why others should buy the coverage.

In 1983, several disgruntled shareholders sued the troubled financial services company for alleged fraud and misrepresentation. Not only that, but they also looked longingly at the personal fortunes of Baldwin-United's wealthy directors and sued them too.

More than 97 percent of all companies of Baldwin-United's size insure their directors against liability in the event they are sued for any decision they make as a board. But Baldwin-United's directors were never insured against this type of liability because the Cincinnati concern promised to pay the expenses of any lawsuits.

The promise was made when the company posted stunning earnings gains. But by 1983, the firm was financially strapped and couldn't pay $1 billion in short-term debt.

By then, it was too late for the directors to get coverage for themselves because they had already been sued by the stockholders. The directors had to sweat it out until December 1986, when a settlement was reached.

BELOW THE LINE

WRITING OFF ETHICS AND MORALITY

When the Government Pulled the Plug on the Great Electrical Conspiracy

It was the biggest criminal case in the history of the Sherman Act, the most infamous antitrust action in the electrical industry.

General Electric, Westinghouse, and twenty-seven other firms were found guilty in 1961 of the price-rigging of $1.75 billion worth of equipment annually for eight years. The companies had conspired to fix prices, rig bids, and divide markets on everything from tiny $2 insulators to multimillion-dollar turbine generators.

Middle-level managers in the industry met regularly to carry out the scheme. For example, the sales of circuit breakers through sealed bids to governmental agencies and private utilities were rotated among four firms on a fixed percentage basis—45 percent for G.E., 35 percent for Westinghouse and 10 percent each for Allis-Chalmers and Federal Pacific. Every ten days to two weeks, the conspirators held meetings—which they fondly called "choir practice"—to decide who was to get the next order and for what "low bid."

A second level of conspirators, involving the four companies and many other firms, pulled off their scam with electrical equipment sold to the private sector. Once each week, certain general managers and vice-presidents got word to each other through coded intercompany memos.

The conspirators had their own standard operating procedures to avoid detection. Each company had a code number that was used in all memoranda and phone calls. At hotel meetings, the schemers did not list their employer when registering and were seldom seen dining in public with their fellow conspirators. The G.E. men had two additional precautions—never be the ones who keep the records and never tell the company attorneys anything.

Finally, someone squealed, triggering a massive Justice Department probe and subsequent trial. After the evidence was presented, the court handed out seven jail sentences, twenty-four suspended jail sentences, and nearly $2 million in fines to twenty-nine corporations.

The guilty executives came from middle management. However, Judge J. Cullen Ganey, chief of the U.S. District Court in Philadelphia where the trial was held, said that the "real blame" should be laid at the doorstep of the men in the highest echelons of the companies. "One would be most naive indeed to believe that these violations of the law, so long persisted in, affecting so large a segment of the industry and finally involving so many millions upon millions of dollars, were facts unknown to those responsible for the corporation and its conduct . . ."

For the record, the guilty companies were: Allen-Bradley Co., Allis-Chalmers Manufacturing Co., Carrier Corp., A. B. Chance Co., Clark Controller Co., Cornell-Dubilier Electric Corp., Cutler-Hammer Inc., Federal Pacific Electric Co., Foster Wheeler Corp., General Electric Co., Hubbard & Co., I-T-E Circuit Breaker Co., Ingersoll-Rand Co., Joslyn Manufacturing & Supply Co., Kuhlman Electric Co., Lapp Insulator Co., McGraw-Edison Co., Moloney Electric Co., Ohio Brass Co., Porcelain Insulator Co., H. K. Porter Co., Sangamo Electric Co., Schwager-Wood Corp., Southern States Equipment Corp., Square D Co., Wagner Electric Corp., Westinghouse Electric Co., C. H. Wheeler Manufacturing Co., and Worthington Corp.

A Roster of Wrongdoing

There have been so many crimes in the executive suite that perhaps there should be a Misfortune 500 Most Wanted List.

For decades, newspapers have been filled with tales of business schemes and scandals. How prevalent is corporate corruption? In a study of 1,043 major corporations in the last full decade, 117—or 11 percent—were involved in crime.

The following chart lists the major successful federal criminal cases against these big companies from 1970 to 1980. The chart is limited to five major offenses: bribery (including kickbacks and illegal rebates), criminal fraud, illegal political contributions, tax evasion, and criminal antitrust violations—all undertaken for the benefit of the corporation.

These cases resulted either in conviction on criminal charges or in consent decrees. Many of the defendants were convicted on pleas of nolo contendere (no contest)—tantamount to guilty pleas but often preferred by defendants because it doesn't have the ring of a confession of guilt.

Although the long arm of the law seldom managed to get past the boardroom door, fifty executives from fifteen companies did go to jail. Several companies were multiple offenders. In all, 188 citations are listed in this chart, covering 163 separate offenses.

COMPANY	OFFENSE
Allied Chemical	**1974**—Fixing prices of dyes. Pleaded nolo contendere. **1979**—Tax fraud related to paying kickbacks. Nolo plea on some charges.
Amerada Hess	**1976**—Fixing prices of gasoline. Convicted after trial. Executive acquitted. Conviction was appealed.
American Airlines	**1973**—Illegal campaign contributions of $55,000. Guilty plea. **1975**—CAB charges related to slush fund used for contributions. Settlement. **1977**—SEC charges related to same. Consent decree.
American Bakeries	**1972**—Fixing prices of bread. Nolo plea.
Amer. Beef Packers	**1975**—Company and president charged with defrauding a creditor. Both found guilty on some counts. **1976**—SEC charges related to same matter. Injunction against president.
American Brands	**1978**—James B. Beam subsidiary and two executives charged with bribery of state liquor official. All pleaded guilty.
American Can	**1976**—Company and executive charged with fixing prices of folding cartons. Nolo pleas by both.
American Cyanamid	**1974**—Fixing prices of dyes. Nolo plea.

COMPANY	OFFENSE
American Export Ind.	**1979**—American Export Lines subsidiary charged with fixing prices of ocean shipping. Nolo plea.
Anheuser-Busch	**1977**—SEC charges concerning $2.7 million in payments to customers. Consent decree. **1978**—Treasury Dept. charges about same matter. Settlement and $750,000 fine.
Archer-Daniels-Midland	**1976**—Defrauding grain buyers by short-weighting. Nolo plea.
Arden-Mayfair	**1971**—Company and executive charged with fixing prices of dairy products. Nolo pleas. **1977**—SEC charges related to $4.4 million in rebates and off-book accounts. Consent decree. **1978**—Price fixing of dairy products. Nolo plea.
Armco	**1973–77**—Three cases of fixing prices of steel reinforcing bars. Nolo pleas by company and three executives.
Ashland Oil	**1973**—Illegal political contribution of $100,000. Guilty plea. **1975**—SEC charges about allegedly illegal payments. Consent decree. **1977**—Fixing prices of resins used to make paint. Nolo plea. **1980**—Ashland-Warren subsidiary pleaded guilty in three cases involving bid rigging in highway construction. Fined a total of $1.5 million.
Associated Milk Prod.	**1974**—Illegal political contributions. Guilty plea.
Beatrice Foods	**1974**—Fixing prices of toilet seats. Company and president of Beneke division pleaded nolo. **1978**—SEC charges about improper accounting for $11.7 million in rebates. Consent decree.

COMPANY	OFFENSE
Bethlehem Steel	**1973–74**—Two cases of fixing prices of steel reinforcing bars. Company and one employee pleaded nolo; another convicted after trial. **1980**—Mail fraud related to bribes paid for ship-repair business. Guilty plea.
Boise Cascade	**1978**—Fixing prices of corrugated containers. Nolo pleas by company and two plant managers.
Borden	**1974 & 1977**—Two cases of fixing prices of dairy products. Company and three executives pleaded nolo.
Borg-Warner	**1971**—Fixing prices of plastic pipe fittings. Nolo plea.
Braniff International	**1973**—Illegal political contribution of $40,000. Guilty pleas by company and chairman. **1975**—CAB allegations about contribution. Settlement. **1976**—SEC charges related to $900,000 slush fund and contributions. Consent decree. **1977**—Criminal restraint of trade. Nolo plea.
CPC International	**1977**—Fixing prices of industrial sugar. Nolo plea.
Carnation	**1971**—Fixing prices of dairy products. Company and executive pleaded nolo. **1973**—Illegal political contributions of $9,000. Company and chairman pleaded guilty. **1974**—Fixing prices of dairy products. Nolo pleas by company and general manager.
Carter Hawley Hale	**1974**—Bergdorf Goodman subsidiary charged with fixing prices of women's clothing. Company and executive pleaded nolo.

COMPANY	OFFENSE
Ceco	**1973–77**—Three cases involving fixing prices of steel reinforcing bars. Company and one executive pleaded nolo; another executive convicted after trial.
Celanese	**1971**—Fixing prices of plastic pipe fittings. Company pleaded nolo; executive acquitted.
Cenco	**1976**—SEC charges related to falsifying inventory. Seven of eight former executives signed consent decrees. **1979**—Seven executives indicted on criminal charges of mail fraud related to the same scheme. Three pleaded guilty, three convicted after trial, and one acquitted of fraud charges. Convictions were appealed.
Champion Intl.	**1974**—Bid rigging in purchase of timber from public lands. Company found guilty after trial. Executive acquitted. **1976**—Fixing prices of folding cartons. Nolo plea.
Chemical New York	**1977**—Chemical Bank charged with violations of Bank Secrecy Act in scheme by two branch officials to launder money for alleged narcotics dealer. Officials pleaded guilty to tax charges and company to reduced charges.
Chicago Milwaukee	**1976**—SEC allegations of improper use of assets and political contributions. Consent decree.
Combustion Engin.	**1973**—Fixing prices of chromite sand. Company and executive pleaded nolo.
Consolidated Foods	**1974**—Fixing prices of refined sugar. Nolo plea.
Continental Group	**1976**—Fixing prices of paper bags. Company and one executive convicted after trial; two others acquitted. Company fined $750,000.

COMPANY	OFFENSE
Cook Industries	**1976**—Defrauding grain customers by short-weighting. Company pleaded nolo and five executives pleaded guilty.
Dean Foods	**1977**—Price fixing of dairy products. Nolo pleas by company and executive.
Diamond International	**1974**—Illegal campaign contributions of $6,000. Company and executive pleaded guilty. **1974**—Fixing prices of paper labels. Nolo pleas by company and two executives. **1976**—Fixing prices of folding cartons. Company and seven executives pleaded nolo.
Diversified Industries	**1976**—SEC charges related to alleged short-weighting of customers in metal-recovery processes. Consent decree.
Du Pont	**1974**—Fixing prices of dyes. Nolo plea.
Equity Funding	**1973**—SEC charges relating to $2 billion in fictitious insurance policies. Consent decree. **1973**—Former chairman and 21 other former executives charged with fraud. All pleaded guilty to some counts.
FMC	**1976**—Fixing prices of persulfates. Company and executive pleaded nolo.
Federal Paper Board	**1976**—Fixing prices of folding cartons. Company and two executives pleaded nolo.
Federated Dept. Stores	**1976**—I. Magnin subsidiary charged with fixing prices of women's clothing. Nolo plea.
Fibreboard	**1976**—Fixing prices of folding cartons. Company and executive pleaded nolo.

COMPANY	OFFENSE
Firestone	**1976**—SEC charges about slush fund and allegedly illegal political contributions of $330,000. Consent decree. **1979**—False tax-return charges related to $13 million in set-aside income. Guilty plea on some counts.
Flavorland Industries	**1979**—Fixing prices of meat. Nolo plea.
Flintkote	**1973**—Fixing prices of gypsum board. Company, chairman, and president pleaded nolo.
Franklin New York	**1974**—SEC charges against nine executives relating to the bankruptcy of Franklin National Bank. Company and eight executives signed consent decree. **1975**—Eight former executives and employees of bank charged with fraud. All pleaded guilty. **1978**—Three other former executives charged with fraud. All convicted after trial.
Fruehauf	**1975**—Company, chairman, and vice-president charged with criminal tax evasion. All convicted after trial.
GAF	**1974**—Fixing prices of dyes. Nolo plea.
GTE	**1977**—SEC charges relating to political contributions and payments to local officials. Consent decree.
General Dynamics	**1977**—SEC allegations of improper accounting to disguise political contributions. Consent decree.
General Host	**1972**—Fixing prices of bread. Nolo plea.
General Tire & Rubber	**1976**—SEC charges concerning slush fund and allegedly illegal political contributions. Consent decree.
Genesco	**1974**—Fixing prices of women's clothing. Nolo plea.

COMPANY	OFFENSE
Gimbel Bros.	**1974 & 1976**—Saks & Co. subsidiary charged with two cases of fixing prices of women's clothing. Company and executive pleaded nolo.
B. F. Goodrich	**1978**—Tax evasion related to slush fund used for illegal political contributions. Nolo plea by company; charges against an executive dropped.
Goodyear	**1973**—Illegal political contribution of $40,000. Company and chairman pleaded guilty. **1977**—SEC charges concerning slush fund of $500,000 for contributions. Consent decree.
Great Western United	**1974**—Great Western Sugar subsidiary charged with fixing prices of refined sugar. Nolo plea.
Greyhound	**1974**—Illegal campaign contributions of $16,000. Guilty plea.
Gulf Oil	**1973**—Illegal political contributions of $100,000. Company and executive pleaded guilty. **1975**—SEC charges about $10 million slush fund used for political contributions. Consent decree. **1977**—Company and two employees charged with giving illegal gifts to an IRS agent. Company pleaded guilty, one employee pleaded nolo, the other convicted after trial. **1978**—Fixing prices of uranium. Pleaded guilty.
Hammermill Paper	**1978**—Palmer Paper Co. unit charged with fixing prices of paper products. Company and executive pleaded nolo.

COMPANY	OFFENSE
Heublein	**1978**—Bribery of state liquor official. Guilty plea.
Hoerner Waldorf	**1976**—Fixing prices of folding cartons. Company and four executives pleaded nolo. **1978**—Fixing prices of corrugated containers. Nolo plea.
ITT	**1972**—ITT Continental Baking subsidiary charged with fixing prices of bread. Nolo plea.
Inland Container	**1978**—Fixing prices of corrugated containers. Nolo plea by company and executive.
International Paper	**1974**—Fixing prices of paper labels. Company and two executives pleaded nolo. **1976**—Fixing prices of folding cartons. Company and four executives pleaded nolo. **1978**—Fixing prices of corrugated containers. Nolo plea. Fined $617,000.
Walter Kidde	**1977**—SEC charges against U.S. Lines subsidiary related to $2.5 million in allegedly illegal rebates. Consent decree. **1978**—Federal Maritime Commission charges related to same. Settlement. **1979**—U.S. Lines charged with fixing prices of ocean shipping. Nolo plea. Fined $1 million.
Koppers	**1979**—Bid rigging in connection with sale of road tar to State of Connecticut. Nolo plea.
LTV	**1978**—Agriculture Dept. charges against Wilson Foods subsidiary related to alleged illegal payoffs to customers. Settlement.
Liggett Group	**1978**—Paddington Corp. subsidiary charged with bribery of state liquor official. Guilty plea.

COMPANY	OFFENSE
Litton Industries	**1974**—Fixing prices of paper labels. Convicted after trial.
3M	**1973**—Illegal campaign contribution of $30,000. Company and chairman pleaded guilty. **1975**—SEC charges related to $634,000 slush fund for contributions. Consent decree.
Marcor	**1976**—Container Corp. subsidiary charged with fixing prices of folding cartons. Company and eight executives pleaded nolo. **1978**—Subsidiary charged with fixing prices of corrugated boxes. Company and two executives pleaded nolo.
Martin Marietta	**1978**—Martin Marietta Aluminum subsidiary charged with fixing prices of titanium products. Company and executive pleaded nolo.
Mattel	**1974**—SEC charges related to false disclosures to influence stock prices. Consent decree. **1978**—Former president indicted on criminal charges related to same matter. Nolo plea.
J. Ray McDermott	**1976**—SEC charges related to slush fund of more than $800,000 used for commercial bribes and illegal political contributions. Consent decree. **1978**—Wire fraud and racketeering charges relating to the bribes and contributions. Guilty plea. **1978**—Bid rigging and allocation of contracts relating to pipeline and offshore-oil-rig construction. Company, president, and three other executives pleaded nolo. Company fined $1 million.
Mead	**1976**—Fixing prices of folding cartons. Company and executive pleaded nolo.

COMPANY	OFFENSE
National Distillers	**1978**—Bribery of state liquor official. Pleaded guilty. **1980**—Treasury Dept. allegations of illegal payments to customers. Settlement and $750,000 fine.
Northern Natural Gas	**1972**—Mail fraud related to bribery of local officials to obtain right-of-way permits for pipeline construction. Company and one executive pleaded nolo to some counts; charges against another executive dropped.
Northrop	**1974**—Illegal campaign contributions of $150,000. Company and two executives pleaded guilty. **1975**—SEC charges related to slush fund for $500,000 in domestic contributions. Consent decree.
Occidental Petroleum	**1974**—Illegal campaign contribution of $54,000. Executive and later the chairman pleaded guilty. **1977**—SEC charges related to $200,000 slush fund for contributions in the U.S. and abroad. Consent decree.
Olinkraft	**1978**—Fixing prices of corrugated containers. Company and one executive pleaded nolo; another executive acquitted.
Owens-Illinois	**1978**—Fixing prices of corrugated containers. Company and one executive pleaded nolo; two others acquitted.
Pan American	**1975**—Illegal fare cutting. Nolo plea. **1977**—Fixing prices of military fares. Nolo plea.
Peavey	**1977**—Defrauding grain customers by short-weighting. Nolo plea.
Penn Central	**1974**—SEC charges of fraud relating to the bankruptcy of the railroad. Consent decree.

COMPANY	OFFENSE
PepsiCo	**1970**—Frito-Lay subsidiary charged with fixing prices of snack food. Nolo plea. **1977**—Parent company charged with fixing prices of industrial sugar. Nolo plea. **1979**—Parent company and two executives of Monsieur Henri subsidiary charged with bribing a union official. All pleaded guilty.
Pet	**1970**—Fixing prices of snack foods. Nolo plea.
Phillips Petroleum	**1973**—Illegal campaign contribution of $100,000. Company and chairman pleaded guilty. **1975**—SEC charges related to $2.8 million slush fund, a portion of which was allegedly used for domestic illegal political contributions. Consent decree. **1975**—Fixing prices of gasoline. Nolo plea. **1976**—Tax evasion related to the slush fund. Guilty plea.
Pittston	**1977**—Brink's Inc. subsidiary charged with bid rigging and fixing prices of security services. Company and five executives pleaded nolo. Company fined $625,000.
H.K. Porter	**1974**—Fixing prices of steel reinforcing bars. Nolo plea.
Potlatch	**1976**—Fixing prices of folding cartons. Company and one executive pleaded nolo; another executive acquitted.
Purolator	**1978**—Bid rigging and allocation of markets for security services. Nolo plea.

COMPANY	OFFENSE
Rapid-American	**1978**—Schenley subsidiary and three executives charged with bribery of a state liquor official. All pleaded guilty. **1979**—SEC charges against Schenley related to $6 million in allegedly illegal payments to customers. Consent decree.
Reichhold Chemicals	**1977**—Fixing prices of resins used to make paints. Company and executive pleaded nolo.
R.J. Reynolds Ind.	**1977**—Federal Maritime Commission charges against Sea-Land Services subsidiary relating to illegal payments to customers. Settlement and $4 million fine. **1978**—SEC suit against Sea-Land related to $25 million in allegedly illegal rebates and political contributions. Consent decree. **1979**—Fixing prices of ocean shipping. Nolo plea. Fined $1 million.
Rockwell International	**1978**—Fixing prices of gas meters. Pleaded guilty.
St. Regis Paper	**1976**—Fixing prices of folding cartons. Company and executive pleaded nolo.
F.&M. Schaefer	**1978**—Treasury Dept. allegations of $600,000 in illegal rebates to customers. Settlement.
Jos. Schlitz Brewing	**1977**—SEC charges related to $3 million in illegal rebates to customers. Consent decree. **1977**—Fixing prices of beer. Company and executive pleaded nolo. **1978**—Treasury Dept. allegations of illegal marketing practices and rebates. Consent decree and $750,000 fine.

COMPANY	OFFENSE
Joseph E. Seagram	**1977**—SEC charges related to over $1 million in allegedly illegal rebates to customers and political contributions. Consent decree. **1978**—Seagram Distillers, three other subsidiaries, and four executives charged with bribery of a state liquor official. All pleaded guilty. **1979**—Illegal payments to members of a state liquor-control board. Guilty plea. Fined $1.5 million.
Seatrain Lines	**1978**—Payment of illegal rebates and violation of currency regulations. Guilty plea in criminal case and $2.5 million fine paid in Federal Maritime Commission case. **1979**—Fixing prices of ocean shipping. Nolo plea. **1980**—SEC suit related to $14 million in rebates to customers. Consent decree.
Singer	**1975**—Illegal campaign contribution of $10,000. Guilty plea.
SuCrest	**1977**—Fixing prices of industrial sugar. Nolo plea.
Tenneco	**1976**—Packaging Corp. subsidiary charged with fixing prices of folding cartons. Company and four executives pleaded nolo. **1978**—Mail fraud in connection with bribery of a local official. Guilty plea.
Textron	**1978**—Fixing prices of gas meters. Pleaded guilty.
Time Inc.	**1976**—Eastex Packaging subsidiary charged with fixing prices of folding cartons. Nolo plea.

COMPANY	OFFENSE
Trans World Corp.	**1975**—TWA charged with illegal fare cutting. Nolo plea. **1977**—Fixing prices of military fares. Nolo plea.
Uniroyal	**1977**—SEC charges related to allegedly illegal political contributions. Consent decree.
United Brands	**1975**—SEC charges related to improper use of funds to pay a $1.2 million bribe to a Honduran official. Consent decree. **1978**—Wire fraud charges related to the same matter. Guilty plea.
U.S. Steel	**1973**—Fixing prices of steel reinforcing bars. Company and an executive pleaded nolo.
Jim Walter	**1978**—Knight Paper subsidiary charged with fixing prices of paper products. Company and executive pleaded nolo.
Ward Foods	**1972**—Fixing prices of bread. Nolo plea. **1978**—Fixing prices of meat. Nolo plea.
Weyerhaeuser	**1976**—Fixing prices of folding cartons. Company and three executives pleaded nolo. **1978**—Fixing prices of corrugated boxes. Company pleaded nolo, fined $632,000. Two executives acquitted.
Wheelabrator-Frye	**1976**—A. L. Garber subsidiary charged with fixing prices of folding cartons. Nolo plea.
Zale	**1977**—SEC charges related to slush fund to reimburse executives for political contributions. Consent decree.

Chart reprinted by permission of *Fortune*; from an article "How Lawless Are Big Companies?" by Irwin Ross; © 1980 Time Inc. All rights reserved.

A Standard and Poor Policy

How did E. F. Hutton, when it was Wall Street's fifth-largest brokerage firm, manage to enjoy hundreds of millions of dollars in interest-free loans from 1980 to 1982?

By kiting checks. Hutton deposited funds in about 400 commercial banks. After overdrawing an account at one bank, Hutton paid the overdraft by writing another check, which overdrew an account at another bank. With some quick moves, Hutton stayed one step ahead of the bankers and, in effect, obtained an interest-free loan of up to $250 million. However, this type of banking is illegal, and, when the Justice Department spoke up, E. F. Hutton listened. In 1985, the company pleaded guilty to an astounding 2,000 counts of mail and wire fraud. It was fined $2 million plus $750,000 in court costs and ordered to repay the banks $8 million in lost interest.

It Leaves a Bad Taste in Your Mouth

No product has brought more worldwide embarrassment to Colgate-Palmolive than Darkie toothpaste.

Manufactured by a company that is 50 percent owned by Colgate, the toothpaste has been a big seller in Southeast Asia for the past sixty years. Colgate's shame has nothing to do with the toothpaste—other than its racist name and carton.

The box features a caricature of a white American minstrel in blackface. The man in the drawing wears a top hat and flashes a glittering smile.

The fluoridated toothpaste is made by Hawley & Hazel Co., a Hong Kong–Taiwanese firm half owned by Colgate.

When the Interfaith Center on Corporate Responsibility first protested against Darkie in 1985, Colgate claimed that although the name and box might be unacceptable by American standards, Asians saw no slur. "We're not insensitive, but as far as we can determine, it's not racially offensive in the countries where it's sold," said Gavin Anderson, director of international corporate development. "Darkie toothpaste has been sold since the 1920s and was marketed this way as a compliment to Al Jolson."

But the Interfaith Center didn't buy the reasoning. Said executive director Timothy Smith, "If Darkie toothpaste isn't insulting in Asia, then why not sell Chink toothpaste in Europe?"

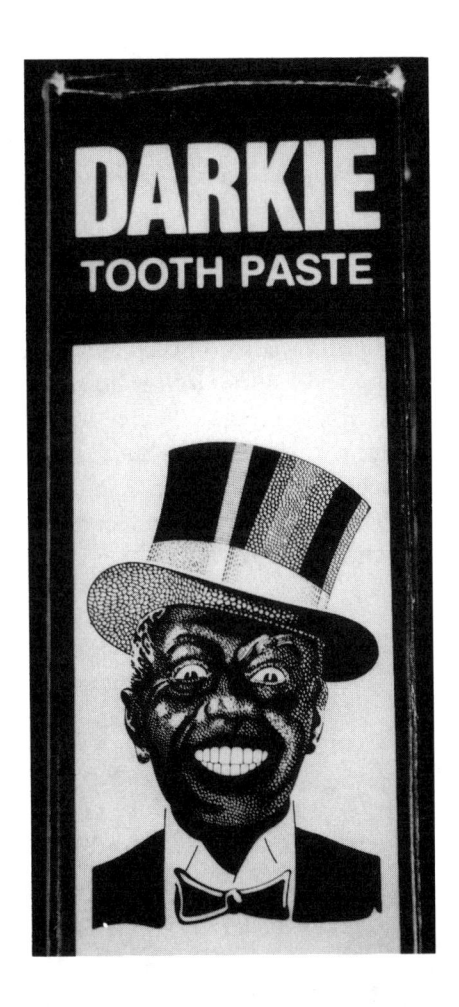

Colgate agreed to modify the Darkie logo and find a new name. The company said the new carton might feature a young, modern, well-dressed black and the new name might be "Dakkie" or "Hawley." However, Colgate is reluctant to change the name or box too much, for fear of losing brand recognition of its best-selling Asian product.

GM's Sacking of Poletown

CHAPTER 1
General Motors insists that Detroit raze a section of the city called Poletown to make way for a highly automated plant to produce luxury cars. The 3,400 residents of the integrated lower-middle-class community launch a protest in 1981, but to no avail.

CHAPTER 2

With GM pulling the strings, the city fathers arrange for $220 million in government subsidies to buy the land, relocate the residents, and demolish the structures. In a last-ditch effort, the Poletown Neighborhood Council pickets GM, then leads a caravan to the home of GM chairman Roger Smith to ask him to give up *his* home and acreage for the plant. Smith is not at home at the time.

CHAPTER 3

Reverend Joseph Karasiewicz, pastor of the Church of the Immaculate Conception, begs Smith in a letter not to tear down the twelve churches in Poletown. Smith does not respond. Father Joe tells the press that destroying churches and a community to build a factory doesn't even happen in communist Poland. Adds a resident, "We are neighbors. We help and love each other. I'll bet those General Motors executives don't have neighbors who love them."

CHAPTER 4

Six months later, a chain is tied to the door of Father Joe's church and a tow truck rips it out. Police in full gear rush into the church basement and arrest a dozen parishioners who had maintained a vigil there to protect their church. Within a few hours, the steel ball of a giant wrecker crashes again and again into the sides of the rectory. Said a policeman who was involved, "You've got to feel bad for the little people—a big corporation like General Motors coming in and pushing them all out."

CHAPTER 5
Charles Mistele, owner of a fuel supply company in Poletown, asks the city to grant him six more months to relocate his firm. Pressed by GM, City Hall says no; GM wants the plant ready in two years. (It took five years to complete the plant.) Mistele is forced to close down, eliminating seventy-two jobs. "I'm bitter," he says. "I've been in business a long time. I'm a private corporation and I've been put out of business just for them."

CHAPTER 6
After the destruction of twelve churches, hundreds of homes and buildings, and the ouster of thousands of residents, GM levels 465 acres of Poletown—and builds a seventy-acre plant.

Reworking Chapter 11
4 Companies That Abused the U.S. Bankruptcy Laws

TEXACO
1987: The nation's third-largest oil company used Chapter 11 bankruptcy filing—designed to protect struggling companies from creditors—to free itself from putting up a $10.5 billion bond. The profitable Texaco sought refuge in bankruptcy court in its bitter fight with Pennzoil over ownership of Getty Oil Co. Pennzoil, which had sued Texaco for interfering in the purchase of Getty, won an $11 billion judgment against Texaco in a 1985 jury decision. A settlement was being hammered out in 1988.

A. H. ROBINS
1985: As lawsuits over its Dalkon Shield intrauterine birth-control device mounted, Robins filed for Chapter 11 protection. The move immediately halted about 5,100 pending lawsuits filed by women who contended that the IUD caused sterility and miscarriages. The Richmond, Virginia–based company says it has set up a fund to cover the claims once it emerges from reorganization.

CONTINENTAL AIRLINES
1983: Frank Lorenzo used Chapter 11 proceedings to rid his airline of burdensome labor contracts. He convinced the bankruptcy court to cancel contracts with three labor unions. Ever since Continental emerged in 1986 from reorganization, its employees have received substantially less pay and fewer benefits, while operating under stricter work rules than before.

MANVILLE CORP.

1982: Formerly Johns-Manville, the company was the first major corporation to abuse the bankruptcy laws, when it sought Chapter 11 protection despite $2 billion in assets. The Denver-based company, once the leading U.S. producer of asbestos, filed for reorganization after it estimated it would be sued by tens of thousands of people claiming their health was endangered by the fireproofing product. The filing froze some 16,500 claims. Manville's reorganization plan, which calls for a $2.5 billion payout to claimants over the next twenty-five years, has been stalled by two lawsuits.

NO-ACCOUNT ACCOUNTING

BEAN-COUNTER CHICANERY

Padding Expenses

EXAMPLE NO. 1
Charter Co., the insurance and oil company, headed for a Chapter 11 bankruptcy filing in 1984 while it was still getting bills from some fancy addresses.

Among the list of creditors were the Hotel Ritz in Paris, pricey New York stores such as Tiffany and Steuben Glass, and cruise-ship operator Cunard Lines Ltd. There were also entertainment bills from Walt Disney World in Florida, Circle Repertory Company in New York, the Los Angeles Rams, and several private clubs in the Jacksonville, Florida area.

A Charter spokesman said the expenditures were part of the company's "routine business and entertainment expenses."

EXAMPLE NO. 2
General Dynamics, the nation's largest defense contractor, charged the Pentagon in 1985 for such items as an $18,000 country-club initiation fee and kennel costs for an executive's dog. These were listed under "overhead costs" that the Pentagon claimed were part of $75 million in unnecessary overcharges. Defense Secretary Caspar Weinberger was so incensed that he suspended payments to General Dynamics for several weeks—a punishment that cost the company $40 million a month.

"...AND, SINCE FIFI'S KENNEL DOES HAVE A ROOF, I THINK WE CAN HONESTLY CALL HER BOARDING FEES AN 'OVERHEAD COST'..."

EXAMPLE NO. 3
Northwest Energy Co., the Salt Lake City concern that headed the Alaska pipeline consortium, tried in 1981 to pass on to prospective customers more than $1 million for nonconstruction activities since the mid-1970s. For example: $20,000 "for a chartered fishing trip and riverboat reception" before a business meeting; $19,000 for parties in Washington, D.C., "to celebrate President Carter's selection" of the route for the project; $13,000 to cover membership dues for "various country clubs, luncheon and dinner clubs and athletic clubs"; $14,450 for providing ski lessons and more "fishing arrangements" for various officials; and $3,658 "to satisfy the Oriental business custom of exchanging gifts" with business associates. The company said it considered "all of them to be legitimate business costs." Auditors for the Federal Energy Regulatory Commission disagreed.

EXAMPLE NO. 4
Northrop was shot down by government auditors who demanded

reimbursement of millions of dollars worth of company charges for questionable overhead expenses, including entertainment of Defense Department personnel. Included in the "overhead" was a Maryland duck-hunting lodge that the company leased. Northrop hosted more than 140 weekends there for Pentagon brass between 1971 and 1974.

Forget the Math Skills, Can You Write Fiction?

Creative accounting involves much more than just juggling numbers. It also requires writing skills.

The Cleveland-based accounting firm of Ernst & Whinney—one of the nation's largest—found itself in trouble in 1983 when the Justice Department filed a civil lawsuit against the company on behalf of the Internal Revenue Service. The government accused the firm of intentionally using "false, misleading and deceptive" terms in a "word game, a verbal sleight of hand."

According to the suit, Ernst & Whinney tried to rename the parts of a new building in order to obtain investment tax credits for a client. Among the cleverly created terms the firm coined were:

- *combustion enunciator*—fire alarm bell
- *movable partitions*—doors
- *decorative fixtures*—windows
- *freezer*—entire refrigerated warehouse
- *identifying devices*—fifty-foot-high shopping-center signs
- *planter*—thirty-two tons of gravel and ninety-two cubic yards of topsoil.

Ernst & Whinney, in its court papers, said the vocabulary was used "to put the client's best foot forward." In so doing, the firm slipped and fell flat on its face.

A Citicorp Tragicomedy

CHAPTER 1
Citicorp—the nation's second largest bank holding corporation—is told in 1982 by one of its own officers that the bank's branches in Europe are illegally transferring money to tax-free and tax-reduced accounts in the Bahamas to avoid the tax and currency laws of foreign countries.

CHAPTER 2
A dispute arises within the Securities and Exchange Commission over Citicorp's improper currency transactions. Some staffers want sanctions against Citicorp. But others say they do "not subscribe to the theory that a company that violates tax and exchange control regulations is a bad corporation." SEC's chief of enforcement, John Fedders, argues that even if the transactions are illegal, they constitute a "standard business judgment" to try to maximize profits.

CHAPTER 3
A majority of the five SEC commissioners agree with the novel argument that Citicorp management has no legal duty to disclose the improper transactions, because the firm never represented to stockholders that its top officers possessed "honesty or integrity." The SEC decides to take no action because the case involves banking and taxes, not securities.

CHAPTER 4
Citicorp officer David Edwards, who first told the bank's senior management of the irregularities, is fired.

Corporate Accountability

General Dynamics Corp., the nation's largest military contractor, did not pay any federal income tax from 1972 to 1986, even though the company reported more than $2 billion in profits during that time. Because the firm used an accounting method called "completed contract accounting," it was able to pay dividends of more than $100 million to its shareholders—dividends that were not taxable.

AT&T disputed a study in 1986 that revealed that the giant multibillion-dollar corporation had paid no income tax. AT&T cited a special provision of the tax code, which stated that a growing company may defer paying taxes until later years. Thus, a firm that continues to grow may defer paying taxes forever. AT&T contends that it's a growing firm and, thus, deferred taxes should be counted as taxes actually paid.

Tenneco Inc. announced in 1986 that it would change its accounting methods and would take $988 million in charges against prior years' earnings. Accounting experts hailed the ploy as a "cleverly timed change" and "creative accounting."

The Penrod Drilling Co., an oil company owned by the Hunt brothers, made money in 1985 despite posting losses of more than $100 million. Isn't it amazing what accounting can do?

A CROCK FOR YOUR STOCK

CORPORATE ABUSE OF SHAREHOLDERS

Do You Get the Feeling We're Not Welcome Here?
How Companies Stifle Shareholders' Voices at Annual Meetings

Fuqua Industries swept through its 1986 annual meeting in just two minutes. Only three people showed up. The firm's president, Lawrence P. Klamon, claimed shareholders were so pleased with the company's performance that they didn't bother to attend. Perhaps a better reason was Fuqua's habit of scheduling annual meetings early on Saturday mornings. The company record for the shortest annual meeting is one minute, fifty seconds, set by chairman J. B. Fuqua in 1973 after the New York Stock Exchange refused his request to discontinue annual meetings.

Sierracin Corp., an aerospace subcontractor, restricted attendance at its 1986 annual meeting to shareholders only because it was being held in the company's 200-seat cafeteria. When an attorney for one of the stockholders wanted to accompany his client, the company refused to let the lawyer in. So the attorney bought a share from another stockholder and got inside—to find only twenty shareholders in attendance. During the meeting, stockholders had questions about an unusual corporate self-insurance plan and two lawsuits against the firm. The officers refused to answer any questions because, they told the shareholders, it was company policy not to entertain questions at annual meetings.

"WELL, IF THERE ARE NO QUESTIONS FROM THE FLOOR, I GUESS I'LL ADJOURN THE MEETING."

Standard Brands tried to thwart stockholder participation during its 1960 annual meeting by holding the affair in a large room without microphones. Stockholders were unable to make themselves heard and could not hear what was going on. Before the meeting, management had also announced that it would answer only questions submitted in writing, permitted no rejoinder to the answers, and refused to consider a raft of complaints about the whole procedure.

Swan-Finch had a history of pulling the welcome mat out from under its shareholders. The man most responsible was its embattled chairman Lowell Birrell, who was accused of involvement in several corporate swindles. To avoid a stockholder revolt over his alleged schemes, Birrell scheduled the annual meeting for the Fourth of July weekend when most people would be vacationing. A few years later, he tried to cut short an annual meeting held in the summer by closing the windows and turning off the air conditioning.

IBM and its chairman Thomas Watson, Jr., believed in cutting off the speaker by cutting off the microphone. But that tactic didn't always work. During the company's annual meeting in 1966, Watson cut off activist stockholder Wilma Soss in midsentence as she was making a particularly unappreciated point. Not to be outdone, Soss whipped out a megaphone from her raincoat and continued her tirade without missing a beat. Watson retaliated by ordering her bodily removed from the meeting. Five years later, he had three Pinkerton guards throw Soss out again while she was criticizing a board member.

Chase Manhattan Bank had a history of packing annual meetings with loyal employees, ready to hoot and jeer minority stockholders who disagreed with the company's views. A favorite tactic of chairman Winthrop Aldrich was to embarrass people speaking from the floor by asking how many shares they represented. The fewer the shares, the louder the laughter. This ploy was stopped after Aldrich tangled with Lewis Gilbert, a champion of the stockholder. When Aldrich asked Gilbert how many shares he had during an annual meeting, Gilbert shot back, "That's an improper question. I must ask you to withdraw it. The law states—and you should know it—that I have as much right to ask questions as the owner of 10 shares as I would have if I owned 10,000 shares." Aldrich apologized.

Genesco tried to keep shareholders in the dark during its annual meetings in the early 1970s. The proceedings were held in a theater that had ample lighting on the dais. However, it was so dark in the audience that shareholders could not read or take notes.

Public Service Co. of Colorado put stockholders through an endurance test, designed to wear them down and keep them from speaking out at its annual meeting in 1969. The company subjected the audience of several hundred shareholders to hours and hours of a boring slide show of historic lanterns, a film on the construction of the utility's nuclear plant, and long-winded monologues by management. The audience became so fatigued that when a stockholder tried to press for some reform proposals, the weary crowd clamored to call it a day— just what the company had hoped for.

Management by Objections

How Chairmen Responded to Shareholder Criticism

Chock Full o' Nuts chairman William Black's response when he was annoyed by stockholders' pointed questions in 1970:

He stormed out to a chorus of boos and never attended another annual meeting of his company.

United States Steel chairman Irving Olds' response when pandemonium among irate shareholders broke out during the 1949 annual meeting:

Olds pounded his gavel with such reckless abandon that he accidentally hammered his own watch into a shapeless mass.

TFI Companies Inc. chairman Herbert Moiner's response during the 1979 annual meeting, when an angry stockholder asked Moiner to justify his $225,016 yearly income and the annual raises given company executives, while stockholders hadn't received a dividend in nine years:

Moiner thanked the stockholder for the "legitimate questions" and, without answering them, dispensed with routine business and abruptly adjourned the meeting.

AT&T chairman Frederick Kappel's response to two stockholders who complained he was violating accepted rules of procedure at the annual meeting in 1965:

"This meeting is not being conducted according to Robert's Rules of Order, but according to my rules. Take your seat or I'll have you thrown out!"

Desilu president Lucille Ball's response during the 1965 annual meeting when activist stockholder John Gilbert charged that Lucy's $500,000 income was equal to the loss the company had sustained:

Lucy became so enraged that her attorney ordered her security man to kick Gilbert out. Unknown to them, Gilbert was a club champion boxer, and he worked over the security man in a bloody, fierce match until Lucy called a recess. Before leaving her seat, she asked sarcastically, "Mr. Gilbert, do you mind if I go to the ladies' room?" Gilbert gave his permission and Lucy stormed out, slamming the door behind her. "This has been a real show," said Gilbert. "Too bad it wasn't on television. It might have increased our revenues."

Have Your Cake and Eat It Too

For annual meetings, Armand Hammer's Occidental Petroleum Corp. takes the cake—literally.

To stifle any management-opposed shareholder resolutions, Oxy has turned its annual meetings into a well-orchestrated 2½-hour birthday party for Chairman Hammer. The event, held on Hammer's birthday, May 21, at a Beverly Hills' hotel, usually includes a "surprise" birthday cake followed by long, effusive speeches and a thirty-minute company film that praises Hammer's contributions to the arts and to international business.

Hammer has silenced dissident shareholders by having their microphones cut off and in recent years has refused to allow any speeches, remarks, or discussion regarding any shareholder resolutions that he opposes.

Forget the Annual Report, Get Me a Map
Companies That Go Out of Their Way to Hold Annual Meetings

Olin Mathieson Chemical Corp., headquartered in New York, invited its 73,000 stockholders during the early 1960s to attend its annual meetings in Saltville, Virginia, site of the firm's first plant. To get there, stockholders had to fly or take a train to Bristol, Virginia, where they changed to a new train for Glade Spring. Once they arrived in the town, stockholders had to hike nine miles to the plant or pay one of the locals to drive them there because there was no public transportation. The meetings lasted less than an hour and no lunch was served. In 1961, only one hardy shareholder was able to make it to the meeting.

General Host Corp. held its 1967 annual meeting in the middle of the Florida Everglades. The company conducted the affair in an isolated sawgrass and mangrove wilderness camp at the southern tip of the Florida peninsula. Incredibly, forty die-hard stockholders showed up for the meeting. Unfortunately, so did squadrons of hungry mosquitoes and a tropical cloudburst.

Goldfield Corp., a Manhattan-based company with a hankering for solitude, held its annual meetings in Evanston, Wyoming, for more than sixty years. The best way to get there, chairman Richard Pistell once told stockholders, was to "fly to Salt Lake City, then drive up the hill about an hour."

Schlumberger Ltd., the New York oil-field services company, holds its meetings on the Caribbean island of Curaçao, where it is incorporated. In 1984, said a spokesman, the company experienced its "most active meeting in history" when a record number of shareholders were in attendance—two. The low-key affair was held in a notary's conference room in the capital city of Willemstad. None of the eleven outside directors showed up. Neither did chief executive officer Jean Riboud.

Technical Tape, Inc., a New Rochelle, New York, concern, created a tradition of choosing remote spots for its annual meetings. In a five-year period, it held meetings in Carthage, Missouri; Carbondale, Illinois; Brenham, Texas; Cornwall, Ontario, Canada; and Beacon, New York. Just to make it even more inconvenient for shareholders to attend, the company held these meetings on December 28—right in the middle of the holiday season.

Standard Oil of New Jersey used to hold its annual meeting in the uncomfortable and acoustically poor boiler room of its Bayway Refinery.

Syntex Laboratories, a pharmaceutical and manufacturing company with a major plant in California, holds its annual meetings in Panama. Syntex said it has to meet in the Central American country because that's where the company was incorporated. However, Panamanian law states that annual meetings can be held in or out of the country.

BSF Co., a New York investment company, held its annual meetings in the 1960s in the tiny town of Wilmington, Delaware—in a small, one-man office above an abandoned theater.

Two, Four, Six, Eight ... Who Do We Depreciate?

Isuzu Motors set the pace in quickly run annual meetings by hiring goons disguised as pro-management shareholders to intimidate anyone who dared speak up against the company.

Known as *"sokaiya,"* these racketeers are paid to ensure that no note of discord will mar the harmony of the occasion. The Isuzu *sokaiya*'s best performance came during the 1978 annual meeting in Tokyo when the hired guns cheered management's proposals and kept every single critic from reaching the microphone. The meeting was over in twenty minutes.

Japanese authorities say that nearly all corporations listed on the Tokyo Stock Exchange pay *sokaiya* to intimidate stockholders. According to one estimate, such payments in a recent fiscal year totaled more than $600 million.

What company, at its 1965 annual meeting, refused to allow a stockholder to ask a question solely because he was a teenager?

Walt Disney Productions, ironically. Donald Tatum, vice-president of Disney, which has made millions of dollars annually by entertaining young people, would not let fourteen-year-old Mark Greenfield, of Woodland Hills, California, ask a question because Mark was not an adult. Mark, whose stock was held by his mother as custodian, said Tatum's action "was not in good taste for a company like Disney."

What If They Held an Annual Meeting and Nobody Came?

One company learned that the promise of coffee and pastries and a tour of a Brooklyn factory weren't enough to lure stockholders.

For the 1979 annual meeting of the Tensor Corp., the company decided to go out of its way to welcome its shareholders. With the meeting slated to be held in the lamp-making firm's Brooklyn factory, Tensor spent $850 waxing the floors, washing and painting the walls, and even installing an air conditioner. Notices of the meeting went out to all the owners of the 475,000 outstanding shares. Then on the day of the meeting, all the officers of the company put on their best suits and ties and waited and waited . . .

Just one shareholder showed up. "He was in the neighborhood and he came for the danish," Jay Monroe, president of the company, lamented to the press.

The only other people who attended the meeting were the officers, directors, and a few brokers. As a result, the company came up short—by about 20,000 votes—of the required quorum of 50 percent of its outstanding shares.

"We're just going to forget the whole thing," said Monroe.

What international company has a terrorist as a major shareholder?

Fiat, Italy's largest privately owned industrial company. One of its stockholders is none other than the Libyan government of Colonel Muammar Khadafy, which owns 13 percent of Fiat's voting stock and 15 percent of the nonvoting shares—together worth about $2.5 billion.

ARTFUL DODGERS

SIDESTEPPING THE FACTS IN ANNUAL REPORTS

Sneaky Prose and Cons of Annual Reports
How Wily Corporations Conceal Bad News

PENRIL CORP.
In its 1985 AR, the company ignored its consistent decline in net revenues, net income, net per share, and a disastrous 98 percent drop in earnings.

Penril made it tough for shareholders to get a true financial picture by not including the typical percentage-change column and the entire financial highlights listings (items seen in 97 percent of all annual reports). And it simply made no mention of the plunge in earnings.

GENERAL MOTORS CORP.

In its 1986 AR, GM cleverly downplayed the bad news that its net income fell 26 percent, its market share declined 1.5 points, and its costs soared to new heights. It also glossed over the controversial dispute that led to the resignation and buyout of board member H. Ross Perot.

In the report, chairman Roger Smith and president James McDonald wrote in the shareholders' letter of "a carefully drawn strategy" with management that "has moved forward with careful planning and bold actions." GM put the only reference to the Perot mess in a footnote buried on page 37 and briefly mentioned, in small type, GM's repurchase of the shares held by "certain employees and former stockholders [Perot and his associates] for $751.5 million."

KOPPERS CO. INC.

In its 1985 AR, the Pittsburgh construction products and services firm used the Pollyanna approach to explain to its shareholders a $30 million loss, a decline per share from 79 cents to a negative $3.72, and a $138 million charge against pretax income.

Chairman Charles R. Pullin stated in the report, "What may seem at first to be less than good news turns out, in the long run, to be the best of news for shareholders. Consider how [the writeoff] improves our resources for profitable redeployment."

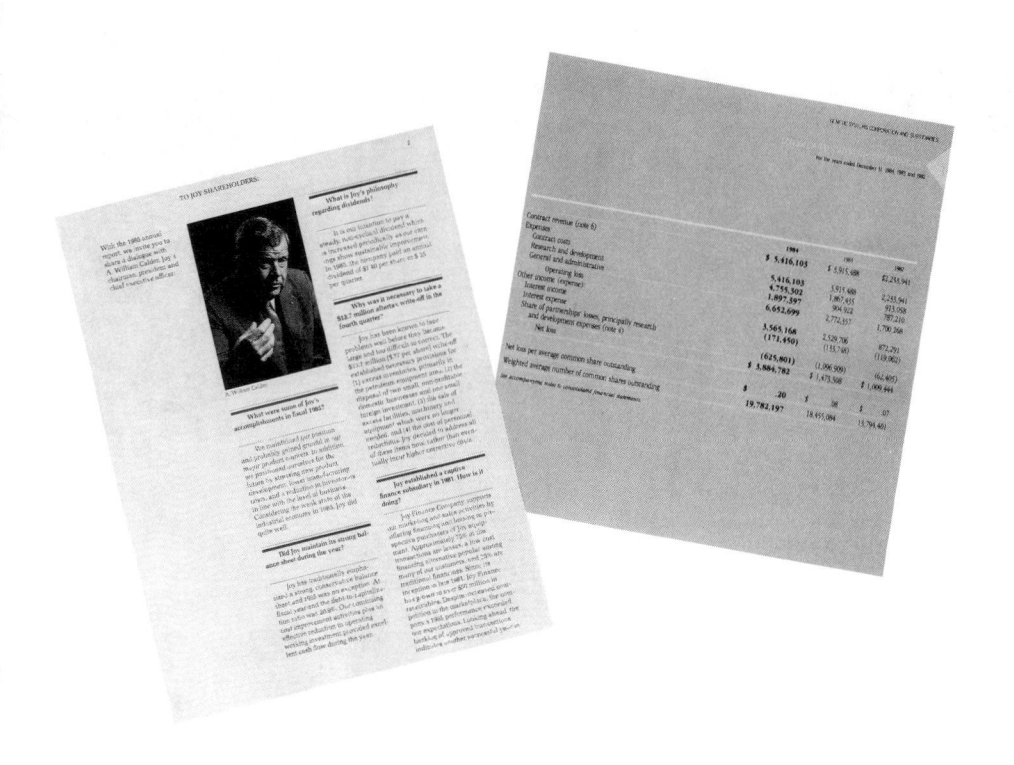

JOY MANUFACTURING

In its 1985 AR, the Pittsburgh-based equipment company tap-danced around an 18 percent increase in sales but a 55 percent drop in net. Here's how the company did it:

The report did not include the usual letter to shareholders. Instead, a new feature was inserted—"Share a Dialogue" with CEO A. William Calder. "Joy has been known to face problems well before they become large and too difficult to correct," he wrote. "We will address all these problems now rather than eventually incur higher corrective costs."

GENETIC SYSTEMS

In its 1984 AR, the biotech company hid the news that its losses were more than twice as great as the year before.

Genetic Systems ignored the financial results in the shareholders' letter and placed the numbers in the back of the report. Instead of using the standard business practice of indicating a loss by putting the figures in parentheses, it showed a category headed "net loss" and ran the numbers without parentheses. It's deceptive but legal.

COLGATE-PALMOLIVE

In its 1984 AR, Colgate-Palmolive slyly downplayed the fact that its earnings plummeted to 86 cents a share from $2.42 the year before, its working capital shrunk alarmingly, and shareholder equity and book value had dropped to the lowest levels since 1979.

CEO Reuben Mark began the shareholders' letter in big, bold lettering by saying, "Colgate-Palmolive today sells over 3,000 products in 135 countries." Readers then plowed through loads of glowing comments before the sixth paragraph disclosed—in lighter, smaller type—the disastrous 1984 earnings numbers. To ease the pain to shareholders, the company enclosed a coupon giving 75 cents off on a new Colgate toothpaste pump containing either the "great regular flavor or Winterfresh Gel."

NATIONAL AIRLINES

In its 1978 AR, National had to explain to shareholders that when one of its Boeing 727 planes crashed and killed three people, the airline made an after-tax insurance profit of $1.7 million on the aircraft. How did National report this tragedy without ever mentioning the fatal accident?

It informed the shareholders that they made an extra 18 cents a share as the result of an "involuntary conversion of a 727."

> What's the simplest way for a company to brush off a $17.4 million writeoff?
>
> Take the audacious approach of David Wallace, chairman of Bangor Punta, who in his letter to stockholders in the company's 1975 AR said, "Needless to say, the writeoff does not mean any cash outlay; it is simply an adjustment to the accounts of the company." Right, and a hanging is merely the placing of a rope around the neck . . .

A Dickens of an Annual Report

How does a company trying to emerge from Chapter 11 handle the news in its annual report? Dynamics Corporation of America turned to Charles Dickens for inspiration. Rather than discuss the facts, DCA's 1975 AR began this way:

"It was the best of times, it was the worst of times, it was the age of wisdom, it was the age of foolishness, it was the epoch of belief, it was the epoch of incredulity, it was the season of Light, it was the season of Darkness, it was the spring of hope, it was the winter of despair, we had everything before us, we had nothing before us, we were all going direct to Heaven, we were all going direct the other way—in short, the period was so like the year 1974 for Dynamics Corporation of America that one might suspect that Mr. Dickens had premonitions of DCA's travail in mind as he started *A Tale of Two Cities*."

Numbers Speak Louder Than Words

On page 1 of the Hydrometals Inc. 1960 AR in bold-face type:
"Your Company Is Now Stronger Financially."
On page 2 in bold-face type:
"Your Company Is Now Stronger Technically."
"Your Company Is Now Stronger in Production."
On page 3 in bold-face type:
"Your Company Is Now Stronger in Management."
"Your Company Is Now Stronger in Marketing."
"Your Company Is Now Stronger in the World Market."
On page 4—at the bottom—in lighter, smaller type:
"This buildup of industrial and commercial strength has endowed your company with capacities which it has never before enjoyed and which, in the judgment of your management, assure its future. Such a process obviously has its cost. In fiscal 1960, the expenses of Hydrometals Inc. exceeded income by $807,390."

> Why was it a bad idea for General Public Utilities to feature its newest nuclear facility on the cover of its 1978 AR?
>
> Because its newest facility was Three Mile Island and the annual report—which boasted that the company's nuclear plants "have an exceptional performance record"—arrived in stockholders' mailboxes the week of the shocking TMI accident.

How to Read Annual Reports

1986 AR: "AM International Inc. enjoyed a year of significant accomplishment in fiscal 1986."

Translation: Net income plunged to $5.7 million from $25.5 million, largely due to a massive restructuring.

1985 AR: Calumet Industries' net income, before an "extraordinary charge of $800,000, reached $1,882,000 or a respectable increase of 13 percent over the previous year's net."

Translation: The company paid $800,000 in a preliminary settlement with the Department of Energy for alleged regulatory violations. This gave Calumet a showing of 81 cents a share, down from $1—a 19 percent decline.

1985 AR: "We have just completed a very important year for CBI Industries—a year in which substantial progress has been made for attaining future profitability."

Translation: On a 63.7 percent revenue increase, per-share net (after asset writedowns) declined 204.3 percent.

1984 AR: "Nineteen eighty-four brought a new beginning for Continental Illinois Corp."

Translation: The Chicago-based banking concern recorded a net loss of $1.1 billion, kicked out five directors and a slew of officers, and was taken over by federal regulators.

1984 AR: Telesphere International's "fiscal 1984 was a year of hard-won progress . . . The company continued to improve its competitive positioning and to lay the base for future profitability."

Translation: Net income plummeted to a $16,042,711 loss from a prior-year profit of $1,080,438.

1983 AR: Champion Parts Rebuilders conceded that "1983 was a tough year."

Translation: How tough was it? Earnings per share dropped about 78 percent—to 21 cents from 97 cents the previous year.

1983 AR: Woods Petroleum Corp. "just completed a year that has required considerable innovation and teamwork on the part of all [our] personnel."

Translation: Revenue declined 11.9 percent while earnings plunged a horrendous 41 percent.

1981 AR: Sambo's Restaurants Inc. "achieved national prominence and publicity."

Translation: The nation's press had reported that Sambo's had filed under Chapter 11 of the Federal Bankruptcy Act.

Mug Shots

Bigwigs at the Chicago financial services company of Walter E. Heller International Corp. had reason to frown over photos of smiling customers featured in its annual reports.

It turned out that two of its clients spotlighted in the 1980 AR were major officers of a Chicago bank that federal regulators forced out of business. And the president of another company that was profiled in the 1980 AR of American National Bank & Trust Co. of Chicago—a Heller unit—was arrested on charges of spying for the Polish government.

What Was That Name Again?

Executive enthusiasm can sometimes get out of hand. Take, for example, Denver-based OEA, Inc., maker of electro-explosive escape-hatch devices. Never heard of the company? That would be a blow to CEO Ahmed Kafadar, who, in the 1986 AR, was afflicted with corporate self-aggrandizement when he told shareholders that "OEA's name is becoming a household word in the U.S. and abroad."

The Wrong Way to Put a Company on the Map

Parker Hannifin Corp., an industrial products maker with more than $1 billion a year in sales, took a little bit too much pride in its worldwide operations.

"Parker's impact is global," boasted the company in its 1981 annual report. "On seven continents, more than 22,000 Parker people are employed . . ."

Well, that was a bit of an overstatement. At the time, Parker did have operations in North America, South America, Europe, Africa, Asia, and Australia. That makes six continents. But the market just wasn't big enough to warrant an office in the world's seventh continent—Antarctica. Said a company spokesman, "Maybe we needed a geography lesson."

Why did Manufacturers Hanover feel compelled to recall its 1981 annual report?

Because the AR stated the company's financial statements had been examined by independent "certified pubic accountants."

WHO'S WHO IN THE MISFORTUNE 500

COMPANIES

Adams Natural Beverage Co., 25
Advance Machine Co., 143
Allegheny International, 6
Allen-Bradley Co., 153
Allied Chemical, 154
Allied Department Stores, 43
Allis-Chalmers Manufacturing Co., 153
Amerada Hess, 54
American Airlines, 140, 154
American Bakeries, 154
American Beef Packers, 154
American Brands, 154
American Can, 154
American Cyanamid, 154
American Export, 155
American Home Products, 71
American Kitchen Foods Inc., 24
American Motors, 16
AmeriTrust Corp., 91, 134
AM International Inc., 195
Anaconda, 16
Anadite Inc., 72
Anheuser-Busch, 92, 138–39, 155
Apple Computer Inc., 91, 126
Arby's, 103
Archer-Daniels-Midland, 155
Arden-Mayfair, 155
Armco, 155
Ashland Oil, 155
Associated Dry Goods, 43
Associated Milk Prod., 155
Atlanta Yellow Pages, 133
AT&T, 56–57, 65, 97, 177, 183
Baldwin-United Corp., 148
Banco Credito y Ahorro Poneeno, 17
BancTEXAS Group, 17
Bangor-Punta, 194
Bank of Boston, 64
Bank of Findley, 78
BBDO-New York, 91
Bear, Stearns & Co., 131
Beatrice, 38, 43, 46, 81, 155
Bethlehem Steel, 16, 156
Beverage Capital Corp., 28
Bloomingdale's, New York, 31
Bohemian Savings & Loan, 77
Boise Cascade, 16, 156
Borden Inc., 130, 156
Borg-Warner, 156
Braniff Airlines, 81, 93, 140, 156
Brunswick, 16
BSF Co., 185

Buick, 68
Burger King, 80
Bushnell, Cruise & Assoc., 126
Cable Electric Co., 114
Calumet Industries, 195
Carnation, 156
Carrier Corp., 183
Carter Hawley Hale, 156
CBI Industries, 195
CBS, 43
Ceco, 157
Celanese, 16, 43, 157
Cenco, 157
Champion International, 157
Champion Parts Rebuilders, 195
A. B. Chance Co., 153
Charter Co., 8, 174
Chase Manhattan Bank, 38, 182
Chemical, New York, 109, 157
Chevrolet, 2–3
Chicago Milwaukee, 157
Chrysler Corp., 16, 89–90, 102, 108–09, 128
Citibank, 109–10
Citicorp, 124, 176–77
Clairol, 28
Clark Controller Co., 153
The Clothing Center, Rochester, NY, 32
Coca-Cola Co., 8–9, 10, 92, 121–22, 136
Coleco Industries, 111
Colgate-Palmolive, 192
Colonial Manor Nursing Home, Youngstown, Ohio, 125
Combustion Engineering, 157
Commonwealth Edison Co., 59, 64
ComputerLand Corp., 12
Conoco, 2
Consolidated Foods, 157
Continental Airlines, 66, 90, 113–14, 142, 148, 171
Continental Group, 157

Continental Illinois National Bank, 55–56, 136, 148
Continental Illinois Corp., 195
Control Data Corp., 66
Cook Industries, 158
Cornell-Dubilier Electric Corp., 153
Corning Glass Works, 83
Corporate Consultants Inc., 66
CPC International, 156
Curtis Publishing, 16
Helene Curtis, 28
Cutler-Hammer Inc., 153
Cuyahoga Group, 88
Dean Foods, 158
Decca Recording Co., 17
Decision Data Computer Corp., 11–12
Delta Rubber Co., 123
Diamond International, 158
Walt Disney Productions, 186
Diversified Industries, 158
Dominion Securities Pitfield Ltd., 134
Douglas Aircraft, 16
Dow Chemical Corp., 63, 73–74
Doyle Dane Bernbach, 86
Du Pont Corp., 18, 158
Du Pont Plaza Hotel, Washington, DC, 115
Dynamics Corporation of America, 194
Eastern Airlines, 90
Eastman Kodak Co., 32, 140–41
Daniel J. Edelman Inc., 73
Elgin National Watch Co., 69
Enteron, 54
Equity Funding, 158
Ernst & Whinney, 176
Fairbanks Whitney, 16
Federal Pacific Electric Co., 153
Federal Paper Board, 158
Federated Department Stores, 158

Fiat, 187
Fibreboard, 158
Firestone, 159
First American Bank of Virginia, 101
First Jersey Securities Inc., 62–63
First National Bank of Chicago, 64
First National Bank of Midland, 17
First National Bank & Trust Co. of Oklahoma City, 17
First Pennsylvania Bank, 131
First Security Bank of Idaho, 131
Flavorland Industries, 159
Flavor Tree, 116
Flintkote, 159
FMC, 34, 36, 158
Ford Motor Co., viii, 9, 16, 27–28, 112–13, 123, 131
Foster Wheeler Corp., 153
Franklin Mint, 66
Franklin National Bank, 159
Frontier Airlines, 113, 142, 148
Fruehauf, 159
Fuji Photo Film Co., 140–41
Fuqua Industries, 180
GAF, 159
General Dynamics, 16, 26, 159, 174, 177
General Electric, 111–12, 152–53
General Foods, 23–24
General Host Corp., 159, 184
General Mills, 104
General Motors, 67, 89, 92, 93, 112, 118, 131, 169–71
General Public Utilities, 65
General Tire & Rubber, 159
Genesco, 16, 159, 182
Genetic Systems, 192
Gerber Products Co., 23
Gillette, 89
Gimbel Brothers, 160

Glenmore Distilleries, 88
GNB Industries, 88
Goldfield Corp., 184
B. F. Goodrich, 160
Goodyear Tire & Rubber, 141, 160
W. R. Grace & Co., 147–48
W. T. Grant, 118
Graphic Scanning Corp., 133
Great Western United, 160
Greyhound, 160
GTE, 159
Gulf Oil, 160
Hammacher Schlemmer & Co., 100
Hammermill Paper, 160
John Hancock Mutual Life Insurance Co., 100
Hanes Hosiery, 116
Harshe & Rotman Inc., 70
Hawley & Hazel Co., 168
Health Valley Natural Foods, 28
Walter E. Heller International Corp., 196
Herbalife International Inc., 62
Heublein Inc., 22, 161
Hewlett-Packard Co., 18, 103
Hoerner Waldorf, 161
Household Finance Corp., 98
Edward Howard & Co., 91
Hubbard & Co., 153
E. F. Hutton, 168
Hydrometals Inc., 194
IBM, 26, 64, 182
Ingersoll-Rand Co., 153
Inland Container, 161
International Harvester, 16
International Paper, 161
International Yogurt Co., 28
Iowa Power & Light Co., 115–16
Isuzu Motors, 186
I-T-E Circuit Breaker Co., 153

ITT, 66, 161
Jac Creative Foods, 28
Jartran Inc., 73
Jheri Redding Products, 28
Joslyn Manufacturing & Supply Co., 153
Joy Manufacturing, 192
Kenner Products, 103
Ketchum MacLeod & Grove, 68
Walter Kidde, 161
King-Seeley Thermos Co., 88
Knight-Ridder Newspapers Inc., 26
Kohlberg Kravis Roberts & Co., 46
Koppers Co. Inc., 161
Kuhlman Electric Co., 153
Lapp Insulator Co., 153
Lettuce Entertain You Enterprises, 55
Lever Brothers, 86
Liggett Group, 161
Lippincott & Margulies Inc., 54
Litton Industries, 162
Lockheed Corp., 16, 59
Louisiana Savings, 97
Lowe's Companies, 104
LTV Corp., 7, 16, 65–66, 161
Luden's Inc., 114
3M, 162
M&M/Mars, 19
Magnussen-Barbee, 96
Manufacturers Hanover Trust Co., 115, 134, 136, 196
Manville Corp., 171–72
Marcor, 167
Martin Marietta, 5, 162
Marvin Les-Lee Appliance, 97
Mattel, 63, 162
MBC Beverage Inc., 104
MCA Inc., 46, 67
MCA Records Canada, 67
J. Ray McDermott, 162

McDonald's Corp., 64, 141
McGraw-Edison Co., 153
Mead, 162
Merrill Lynch & Co., 32
Mesa Petroleum Co., 40–41
Miles Laboratories, 83
Miller Brewing Co., 119, 138–39
MLO Products, 28
Moloney Electric Co., 153
Montgomery Ward, 130
Moody's Investors Service, 136
Morgan Guaranty Trust Co., 71, 111
Mother Jones' Son's Software Corp., 58
Mott's USA, 116
National Airlines, 192
National Bank of Detroit, 115
National Distillers, 163
National Rifle Association, 88
Neenah Foundry, 135
North Carolina National Bank, 77
Northern Natural Gas, 163
Northrop, 163, 175–76
Northwest Airlines, 82
Northwest Energy Co., 175
Northwest Industries, 16
Nybco, 105
Occidental Petroleum Inc., 37, 163, 183
OEA Inc., 197
Ohio Brass Co., 153
Okonite Co., 128
Olinkraft, 163
Olin Mathieson Chemical Corp., 184
Osborne Computer Corp., 72
Owens-Corning Fiberglass Corp., 68–69
Owens-Illinois, 163
Pacific Airlines, 79
Pacific Bell, 115
Pacific Lumber Co., 46

Pan American World Airways, 76–77, 163
Paperback Games, 31
Park Bank of Florida, 17
Parker Hannifin Corp., 197
Peat, Marwick, Mitchell & Co., 66
Peavey, 163
Penn Central, 163
Penril Corp., 190
Penrod Drilling Co., 178
Pepperidge Farm, 31
Pepsico, 8, 9, 90, 92, 121, 136, 143, 164
Pet, 164
Petro-Lewis Corp., 7
Pfeiffers Brewing Co., 91
Phelps Dodge, 120
Philadelphia Electric Co., 132
Phillips Petroleum, 164
Piedmont Airlines, 92
Pittston, 164
Planters Bank, Memphis, 115
Ponderosa, 43
Porcelain Insulator Corp., 153
H. K. Porter Co., 153, 164
Potlatch, 164
Procter & Gamble, 58, 116
Prudential-Bache Securities, 135
Public Service Company of Colorado, 182
Public Service Electric & Gas Co., Newark, 119
Purity Supreme Inc., 104
Purolator, 164
Quaker Bonnet, 28
Rage Music International Inc., 31
Ragu Foods Inc., 82
Ralphs Grocery Co., 71
Ramada Renaissance Hotel, Denver, 96
Rapid-American, 165
RCA Corp., 5, 25–26
Record Bar Inc., 122

Reese Finer Foods Valley Corp., 28
Regency Olds, Lakewood, NJ, 99
Reichhold Chemicals, 165
Remington Arms Co., 18
Republic Airlines, 63
Republic Steel Corp., 146–47
Resort Investment Corp., 96
Revlon Inc., 24, 34, 37, 41, 131
R. J. Reynolds, 165
A. H. Robins, 16, 171
Rocco Enterprises, 119
Rockwell International, 165
Rohr Industries, 16
Rolls Royce Motors Inc., 64, 124
St. Mary's Paper Inc., 123
St. Regis Paper, 165
Saikosha America, 114
Salada Foods Inc., 116
Sambo's Restaurants Inc., 196
Sangamo Electric Co., 153
Sargento Cheese Co., 105
F&M Schaefer, 165
Scheer Advertising, 32
Joseph Schlitz Brewing Co., 10, 89, 165
Schlumberger Corp., 43, 184
Schwager-Wood Corp., 153
Schweppes, 92
Joseph E. Seagram, 166
Seatrain Lines, 166
Sharp, 114
Shell Oil Co., 99
Sierracin Corp., 180
Silo Discount Appliances, 89
Simmons & Co., 28
Singer, 16, 166
Harry Smith Woodworking, 97
Southern States Equipment Corp., 153
South Umpqua State Bank, 77
Sperry, 43
Square D Co., 153

Standard Brands, 181
Standard Oil, 43, 51, 185
States Industries Inc., 88
Studebaker, 16
SuCrest, 166
Sun Oil Co., 65
Swan-Finch, 181
Syntex Laboratories, 185
T. A. Associates, 73
Tatung, 122
Technical Tape Inc., 185
Telesphere International, 195
Tenneco Inc., 166, 177
Tensor Corp., 186
Texaco, 171
Texas Air, 113, 140
Texas Commerce Bancshares, 118
Texas Instruments, 64
Textron, 166
TGI Friday's Inc., 8
J. Walter Thompson, 80, 136
Time Inc., 26, 43, 166
Tobacco Institute, 63
To-Fitness Inc., 28
Trans Florida Airlines, 65
Trans World Corp., 167
TRW, 123
Turtle Wax Inc., 104
UAL Corp., x, 8
Uniden Corporation of America, 103
Uniroyal, 167
Unisonic Products Corp., 114

United Airlines, 78
United American Bank of Knoxville, 90
United Brands, 167
United States Map Co., 103
United States National Bank, San Diego, 17
U.S. Steel, 16, 167, 183
Valvoline Oil Co., 116
Victor Technologies Inc., 96
Wagner Electric Corp., 153
Jim Walter, 167
Ward Foods, 167
Wegmans Food Markets, 65
Weight Watchers, 30
Welk Music Group, 130
Wells Fargo Bank, 99
Western Union Telegraph Co., 18, 51, 133
Westinghouse Electric Co., 152–53
Weyerhaeuser, 167
Wheelabrator-Frye, 167
C. H. Wheeler Manufacturing Co., 153
J. C. Whitney & Co., 105
Wolter Inc., 114
Woodhouse Drake & Carey Inc., 134
Woods & Co., 101
Woods Petroleum Corp., 196
Worthington Corp., 153
Zale, 167

INDIVIDUALS

A. Robert Abboud, CEO First Chicago Corp., 34
Fred Ackman, chairman Superior Oil Co., 35
Bill Agee, president Bendix Corp., 3–5
Winthrop Aldrich, chairman Chase Manhattan Bank, 182
Frank Aldridge, president American Kitchen Foods, 24
Lucille Ball, president Desilu, 183
Michel Bergerac, chairman Revlon Inc., 41–42
Barrie Bergman, chairman Record Bar Inc., 122, 120–23
Lowell Birrell, chairman Swan-Finch, 181
Conrad Black, chairman Argus Ltd., 38
William Black, chairman Chock Full o' Nuts, 182
Ivan Boesky, Wall Street inside trading king, 44
Robert J. Buckley, chairman Allegheny International, 6
August Busch III, president Aneuser-Busch, 139
Willard Butcher, chairman Chase Manhattan, 38
Andrew Carnegie, steel maker, 51
Robert L. Crandall, chairman American Airlines, 140
Mary Cunningham, vice-president strategic planning Bendix, 3–5
Ralph Davidson, chairman Time, 43
J. E. Davis, president Winn-Dixie, 36
Daniel Drew, stock manipulator, 49
James Dutt, chairman Beatrice, 38
Gene Elam, CEO Pacific Lumber, 46
Charles Engelhard, president Engelhard Minerals & Chemicals, 15
Werner Erhard, founder est, 12
Thomas Mellon Evans, chairman Crane Co., 35
Alvin Feldman, president Continental Airlines, 148

Richard J. Ferris, chairman UAL Inc., x
Harry Figgie, Jr., president Figgie International Holdings, 38
Stan Freberg, ad consultant, 79
J. B. Fugua, chairman Fugua Industries, 180
J. Paul Getty, billionaire oil baron, 52
Roberto Goizueta, chairman Coca-Cola, 8
James Goldsmith, corporate raider, 44
Jay Gould, financier, 50
Maurice "Hank" Greenberg, chairman American International Group Inc., 36
Armand Hammer, chairman Occidental Petroleum, 37, 183
Raymond Hay, chairman LTV, 7
Lamar Hunt, oilman, viii, 14–15
Nelson Bunker Hunt, oilman, viii, 14–15
W. Herbert Hunt, oilman, viii, 14–15
Lee Iacocca, chairman Chrysler Corp., 89–90, 147
Richard Jacob, chairman Dayco, 35
Joseph Johnson, chairman Associated Dry Goods, 43
Frederick Kappel, chairman AT&T, 183
Donald Keough, president Coca-Cola, 8
Lawrence Klamon, president Fugua Industries, 180
Jerome Lewis, chairman Petro-Lewis Corp., 7
Frank Lorenzo, chairman Texas Air, 140
Ben Love, chairman Texas Commerce Bancshares, 118
Anthony Luiso, executive vice-president Beatrice, 43
Thomas Macioce, chairman Allied Department Stores, 43
John Macomber, chairman Celanese, 43
Robert Malott, chairman FMC Corp., 34, 36
Matthew McCarthy, president Pacific Air Lines, 79
Richard Melman, president Lettuce Entertain You Enterprises, 55
Bill Millard, founder ComputerLand, 12
John Miller, president Standard Oil, 43
Richard Moe, chairman Delta Rubber Co., 123, 120–23
Herbert Moiner, chairman TFI Companies Inc., 183
John Murphy, president Miller Brewing Co., 139
Bruce Nevins, Adams Natural Beverage Co., 25
Gerald Office, CEO Ponderosa, 43
Irving Olds, chairman U.S. Steel, 183
T. Boone Pickens, chairman Mesa Petroleum, 40–41
Victor Posner, chairman Sharon Steel Corp., 45
Gerald Probst, CEO Sperry, 43
Wallace Rasmussen, chairman Beatrice Foods, 37
Charles Revson, president Revlon, 24, 34, 37

John D. Rockefeller, oil monopolist, 51
Dick Rose, executive Decca Recording, 17
Richard Rosenthal, chairman Citizens Utilities, 37
Daniel Scoggin, CEO TGI Friday's, 8
John Sculley, president Apple Computer, 126
Roger Smith, chairman General Motors, 67, 170, 191
Jim Stevens, Adams Natural Beverage Co., 25
D. J. Sullivan, southern district manager Roadway Express, 36
Donald Tatum, vice president Walt Disney Productions, 186
Donald Trump, president The Trump Organization, 38
Michael Vaillaud, chairman Schlumberger, 43
Cornelius Vanderbilt, shipping magnatc, 49
David Wallace, chairman Bangor Punta, 194
Thomas Watson, Jr., chairman IBM, 182
Thomas Wyman, chairman CBS, 43
Charles Yerkes, transportation magnate, 50

MEMORANDUM

To: The Reader
From: The Authors
Re: Who Else Belongs in The Misfortune 500

    Do you know of any companies or individuals who conduct business like The Misfortune 500? If so, we want to hear about it.
    In this book, we gave you examples of dumb deals, boardroom blockheads, and fiscal fiascoes. But we know that the business world is chock full of more embarrassing and hilarious blunders and gaffes that you never hear about at Harvard Business School. Tell us all about your brainless boss, your competitor's chicanery, or any other funny business you've seen, heard, or read about. Send us a memo (on your company's letterhead if you dare) to:

The Misfortune 500
P.O. Box 31867
Palm Beach Gardens, FL 33410-7867

PHOTO CREDITS

Page 3-No Credit
Page 4-UPI/Bettmann Newsphotos
Page 9-No Credit
Page 10-No Credit
Page 15-UPI/Bettmann Newsphotos
Page 22-New Products Showcase & Learning Center
Page 23-New Products Showcase & Learning Center
Page 24-New Products Showcase & Learning Center
Page 27-Courtesy Perry Piper, The Edsel Owners Club
Page 31-No Credit
Page 44 Left-AP/ Wide World Photos
Page 44 Right-AP/ Wide World Photos
Page 45-AP/ Wide World Photos
Page 49 Left-The Bettmann Archive
Page 49 Right-The Bettmann Archive
Page 50 Left-The Bettmann Archive
Page 50 Right-The Bettmann Archive
Page 51 Left-The Bettmann Archive
Page 51 Right-The Bettmann Archive
Page 52-The Bettmann Archive
Page 56-Courtesy Fallon McElligot
Page 58-UPI/Bettmann Newsphotos
Page 80-AP/ Wide World Photos
Page 98 Top-No Credit
Page 98 Bottom-No Credit
Page 102-Chrysler/Plymouth News Photo
Page 135-Richard Berquist
Page 142-The Denver Post/ Jim Preston
Page 146-LTV Steel
Page 147-AP/ Wide World Photos
Page 169-No Credit
Page 170-The Detroit Free Press/ Craig Porter

DON'T MISS
BRUCE NASH AND ALLAN ZULLO'S

___ THE BASEBALL HALL OF SHAME .... 62062/$6.95

___ THE BASEBALL HALL OF SHAME 2 .... 61113/$6.95

___ THE BASEBALL HALL OF SHAME 3 .... 63386/$6.95

___ THE SPORTS HALL OF SHAME .... 63387/$8.95

___ BASEBALL CONFIDENTIAL .... 65832/$6.95

Simon & Schuster Mail Order Dept. BBB
200 Old Tappan Rd., Old Tappan, N.J. 07675

POCKET
BOOKS

Please send me the books I have checked above. I am enclosing $_____ (please add 75¢ to cover postage and handling for each order. N.Y.S. and N.Y.C. residents please add appro-priate sales tax). Send check or money order--no cash or C.O.D.'s please. Allow up to six weeks for delivery. For purchases over $10.00 you may use VISA: card number, expiration date and customer signature must be included.

Name _____

Address _____

City _____ State/Zip _____

VISA Card No. _____ Exp. Date _____

Signature _____ 173-01